"A must read for anyone needing to find their voice, improve their speaking effectiveness, and market themselves to success."
—Betsy Myers, Founding Director
Center for Women and Business, Bentley University

PITCH PERFECT

Speak to Grow
Your Business in
7 **Simple**
Steps

Mimi Donaldson

Pitch Perfect: Speak to Grow Your Business in 7 Simple Steps
Copyright © 2016 by Mimi Donaldson

ISBN: 978-1-944177-18-8(p)
ISBN: 978-1-944177-17-1(e)

Crescendo Publishing, LLC
300 Carlsbad Village Drive
Ste. 108A, #443
Carlsbad, California 92008-2999

www.CrescendoPublishing.com
GetPublished@CrescendoPublishing.com

A Message from the Author

<u>https://youtu.be/FaioLnV_cMU</u>

To help you get the most value from my book, I'm providing you with some complimentary bonus material, including entertaining, educational audios and videos.

You can download all of these items at:
http://www.pitchperfect.biz

Dedication

To all my speech coach clients, who motivate me, inspire me, and teach me about life.

Thank you to the following for letting me quote your speeches in this book:

Katherine Murray-Morse, Clara Baum, Bridget Stennis, Patricia Pinto, Dorothy Walker Wright, Dan Moriarty and Dr. Tiffany Margolin.

Contents

Part 1
Prepare About Your Audience and More

Part 2
Engage Your Audience with Your Speech

Part 3
Connect with Your Audience on Many Levels

Chapter 1
What This Book Can Do for You

There you are. In an elevator. In a grocery store line. On the sidelines of a kid's soccer field. Someone turns to you and asks, "So, what do you do?" What do you say? Do their eyes light up or glaze over? If they glaze over, I can help with that. That's what this book is all about.

It's also about what you say at a networking meeting when you have only thirty seconds to tell people in the group what you do. They will "ding" you exactly at the thirty-second mark, so every word counts. Some groups give you sixty seconds, but even then, no "ums" or "ahs" will do.

This book will also make it easy to write your ten- or twenty-minute speech to present your products or services in the best light. You will also get this amount of time at your business meeting, Chamber of Commerce meeting, or on the TED Talk stage.

My philosophy is "Build it, and they will come." When you *have* a dynamite speech about your business, opportunities *will* present themselves. You *will* be asked to speak. In this book, consider me your speech coach. My goal is to get you so excited about your speech that you can hardly wait to do it. I want you to be as excited about speaking about your business as you are *about* your business.

If you work for someone else, you'll have an opportunity to improve your presentation skills. Using the speech formula, you will:

- Gain wider acceptance of your ideas
- Get your plans and recommendations implemented more quickly
- Increase the approval rate on your requests for budget, staff, and/or resources

The tips, techniques, strategies and insights in this book will be useful to you, not only in formal business presentations, but also in one-on-one communications, informal small meetings, and even in your family and personal life. Specifically, you will learn how to: Be more comfortable before a group

- Build on your strengths and trust yourself in a group setting
- Organize your material quickly so that it is relevant, interesting, and results-oriented
- Prepare effective visual aids
- Handle questions and answers with grace and control

Learning to be a good presenter is not that difficult. It requires awareness of the dynamics of the communication process, ongoing practice, and, most important, your commitment to using what you learn.

Why Should You Speak?

Speaking can grow your business. Here are five reasons why. You will be able to:

1. Build trust. In today's transparent world, trust is paramount. Customers have to choose a "trusted partner" to engage with. When they hear you speak in front of a group, you have instant credibility because someone has chosen *you* to hold the attention of an audience. Customers feel they can trust you.

2. Reveal your personality. When you speak publicly, you reveal your personality. There is nothing to hide behind. You are speaking about what you know really well, and you can tell stories about problems you've helped to solve. These are true, real-life stories, and some will be humorous. Nothing will sell you like humor.

3. "Sell" your product or service without hard selling. Pointing out the diligent work that clients have thanked you for— even reading a quote from a letter of appreciation—is heartwarming. And the message is loud and clear that you get results because people thank you for your efforts.

4. Spread the word. When you speak for groups, bring cards and brochures (with color pictures) to distribute. You will actually reach more people than are in the audience; people will take your stuff home and share it with others.

5. Give value to get business. Make a useful handout tailored to the majority of your audience members. You've given them a "gift," something of value they can use, and now they are more likely to thank you by giving you something— their business.

Why Do You Need a Speech Coach?

Just as you can't edit your own writing, most of us need help crafting our marketing pitch. I'm having the most exciting, rewarding experiences of my life helping craft business pitches for individuals. I am an educator. The word "educate" comes from "educare," which means "to draw out." I "draw out" all the words that are already inside waiting to be expressed. Good teachers know the student has a lot of innate knowledge; they just need to be drawn out.

Verbal communication is quite different from your website copy. Here are some tips for you, even before I become your formal speech coach:

1. Use short sentences. Your audience is listening, not reading.

2. Right at the start, address a problem they have and how you are uniquely qualified to solve it.

3. Frame your message: Tell 'em what you're going to tell 'em; tell 'em; tell 'em what you told 'em.

4. Follow the listener's train of thought; answer each "yeah, but" that you know is lurking in their minds.

This book offers an easy-to-follow formula that makes it easy to read the minds of your audience.

Before I attended Columbia University Teachers College for my Master's, like so many others, I thought "those who can't, teach." Not true. Those who have spent 10,000 hours mastering a skill (thanks, Malcolm Gladwell) can now teach it. After a training and speaking career of more than thirty years, my biggest thrill comes after reading a note from a client who proudly says, "Did I really say that?" And I smile, nod, and say, "Yes, you did." And they sit a little taller right in front of me, and their eyes get a little brighter. Goose bumps!

Chapter 2
So You Want to Be a Keynote Speaker?

"Motivation will almost always beat mere talent."
– Norman Ralph Augustine

I know it may sound exciting to fly to a great city, stay in a five-star hotel, speak to a thousand people in a hotel ballroom, and get a standing ovation. I've done it for the past thirty years.

But things have changed. Here's the truth: Unless you are already a celebrity, there's only a slight chance you will be a keynoter. In the eighties and nineties, if you were a really good speaker, you could land on a convention program, and you would be paid $5,000 to $10,000. There would be a celebrity speaker who was paid approximately $60,000 to get butts in the seats, and the other speakers would provide the "meat" of the conference.

Now even being a celebrity is not enough. You need national exposure (a platform) with a book or a talk radio or television show—but not a reality show. Notice there is no keynote speaker named Kardashian. Even the "success story" speaker, who has made millions inspiring entrepreneurs and corporate leaders, must now have a book and a hook (i.e., advice on how the audience can "make it big," using the "how-to" method the speaker espouses).

Here's the bottom line: A keynote speech is based on how the speaker's personal experience—their dues-paying activity—can help the audience with a pressing need, problem, or pain that they have right now.

So if you insist that you want to give keynoting a shot, here's how to do it.

First, Pay Your Dues

If you have had teaching or training jobs, you have collected a "body of knowledge." Your speeches can come from that. Here's an example. My first "speech" was actually one hour of a six-hour course called "Communicating for Results" that I taught to first-level and mid-level managers at Northrop Aircraft. The piece that became a "speech" was the hour before lunch, when the managers' attention was at its lowest ebb. It was a piece about the differences between male and female communication—talking and listening.

I had isolated some concepts: how men and women relax, socialize, and bond with their same gender, and the style in which they prefer to give and receive communications. Then I offered real-life examples from their stories—the guys in the class—to illustrate each of my points. (There were no women managers at that time.) It was a laugh riot, and one of the managers asked me to do "that funny part about men and women" for the Management Club, outside class, and I would receive $100. Voila! My first paid speech.

Here's another example. When I first started my own speaking business, I did a lot of management training at a Japanese car manufacturer here in SoCal. I presented full-day trainings on management and presentation skills, among others. At one point, their budget for training had decreased, and they didn't call me for about a year. Then a manager in marketing, not Human Resources, called and asked me to teach "management." At least, that's what I thought he asked. He actually said, "It's a luncheon. You'll have forty-five minutes." I said, "To teach management? You know, I can't change behavior in forty-five minutes." I had created sixty hours of management training that I delivered in four-hour sessions. He said, "That's okay. We don't expect you to change behavior. We

want some TIPS—in your style—you know, entertaining and funny."
Then he quoted what my fee would be, which was *much* more than
their fee for delivering an eight-hour course! I said, "Sure!" and
voila! "Four Steps to Managing Anyone" was born. Still one of my
most popular speeches, it boils down sixty hours of training to four
action steps with riotous, but always true, examples.

So if you have "material," the funny, pithy parts can be distilled into
forty-five–minute keynotes.

The Happiest Person in the Room

Picture this: You are a seasoned speaker. You get to the speaking
venue, and lo and behold, the tables are strewn with litter from last
night's dinner! You know the room has to be totally cleaned and
rearranged for your speech. What would you do? Would you yell
at the hotel staff? Would you find your client and yell at her?

Definitely not. This scenario actually happened to me at an East
Coast hotel early in my career. I sought out the hotel staff and
made SO nice with them they couldn't believe it. I rolled up my
sleeves and worked with them and afterwards gave them free
audiotapes of my funniest speech. The lesson here is: when you
are the speaker, you must be the happiest person in the room, and
the nicest person anyone has ever met. Ever.

No Prima Donnas Here

Years ago, I experienced a wake-up call. I was booked to keynote at
a women's conference at a university known for its great football
team who plays on a blue field. In the preconference phone calls,
the client asked some questions that struck me as very strange.
Her first question was, "Do you require a limo from the airport?"
After finding out the airport was only twenty minutes from the
venue, I told her I didn't even need a hired car; someone could pick
me up, or I would hop into a taxi. She was astonished. "You mean
I could pick you up in my Toyota?" I said, "Sure." She said, "With a
baby seat in the back?" I said, "Sure." She then asked, "What kind
of bottled water do you prefer?" It was the 90's.. I didn't know the

names of bottled water, never mind the differences between them. I said, "I don't care. I usually buy my own water, but it's great that you will provide it."

There was a pause. I asked, "Where are these questions coming from?" She said, "Well, the last speaker we hired from Los Angeles was *very* particular. She insisted on a limo and yelled at the conference volunteer staff when they brought her the *wrong* designer water!" I told her I was shocked. After learning the name of the "speaker/celebrity," I was not that shocked. I assured her, "I am not a diva and I certainly don't *act* like a celebrity, and I'm always very nice to the staff." She sounded relieved. Kudos to the power of kindness!

That was the beginning of my reputation as the "No Prima Donnas Here" speaker. I arrive early, stay after my speech, and *never* bring my wheelie suitcase with me into the speaking room so that I can run away right afterwards. *And*—here's the most important part— if there are speakers before me that day, I attend. There is nothing worse than the third speaker of the day unwittingly contradicting or repeating what a previous speaker said! So be there. Then the audience knows you were there, so they already like you and consider you part of the group.

Be smart. From the moment you enter the taxi on the way to give your speech, all the way through the airport, to everyone with whom you interact, to checking in at the hotel (you never know who may be in the line—once someone recognized my voice from an audiotape she had previously purchased) to dealing with hotel staff, your job is to be *the nicest person anyone has ever met.* Your reputation is all you have, and no one wants a prima donna. Humility is disarming. And it pays off more than you can imagine.

It's Not about You

Do you want repeat business as a speaker? Of course you do. Do you want the client to refer you for other speeches? Of course you do. Both of these goals are achievable only when you focus on the client's needs—not your own. The shift in your orientation is partly a function of maturing as a speaker.

I definitely think there is an "arc" to maturing as a speaker. In the beginning of your speaking career, you draw from your own life experience. In my case, as a Human Resources trainer in a large corporation, I drew my content from the experiences of the managers in my classes. Because I was teaching managers and the courses had to be tailored to their needs, my first really great impactful stories were not about me. They were about the participants: their interactions with uncooperative employees, managing the unmanageable, bringing their stress home and taking it out on their spouses. They were the ones managing people. I was the teacher. So, of course, I used their examples. It had never been about me.

When I transitioned to my own speaking business, I thought I kept up the tradition. I would do a pre-assessment in phone calls with the client to assess their needs and get examples of stress, negotiating situations, or sticky teambuilding issues. I would then incorporate those into my speech.

But more of "me" crept in, and that's how I learned about the "arc" to maturing as a speaker. When I started out in 1984, people came up to me after the speech and said things like: "I want to be you." "Do you need an assistant? I would love to work for you." "Your boyfriend must love you—you understand men so well." It was all about me.

And then about ten years into my career, the comments changed. They were not about me! They became, "You seem to know my husband so well—you must have been in our car," or "I have a story for your speech." They would tell me one of their "aha" moments or funny incidents that I should put in my speech. So it was now about them! And that's when I really started to get referrals and repeat business. (The point? Clients love it when you tailor the speech to their particular needs.) And when it's about "them," they will want you to tailor *another* topic to them. This means more business for you.

After thirty years, I consider it a triumph that it is even *more* about them. People still come up after the speech and say, "I have a story for your speech." But now, in the middle of the speech while I'm talking, they elbow each other and start talking in full voice to each other about what I'm saying on the stage as it relates to them. I love it! Sometimes I stop and just watch and say, "Yes," encouraging them on. Success! The connection to the audience is complete. As a speaker, the connection is your goal in the first place.

So the next time you speak, listen to the comments people give you after you speak. Is it about you, or is it about them? When you are creating your speech, make sure you answer their needs. Then, the only thing "about you" will be the name on the checks they write.

Part 1
Prepare About Your Audience and More

"By failing to prepare, you are preparing to fail."

\- Benjamin Franklin

Chapter3
Prepare About You

"If you do not tell the truth about yourself you cannot tell it about other people."

— Virginia Woolf

We all know how important preparation is before any endeavor. In most things in life, the first thing you need to prepare is *you*. You need to know how you see yourself, face up to how others see you, and develop the skills that will serve you best when you speak to people.

What Gives You the Right?

You can't speak about things you don't know about. In this sophisticated time of TED Talks and YouTube presentations, people seek out experts. Your job is to match your background, dues-paying activity, and formal credentials to the needs of people right now. Your clients and customers have three basic needs:

1. More money

2. More health

3. More love, sex, and communication

Your job is to match your expertise with your potential customer's need. Here's an example: You may want to speak on health because you're a healer or health coach. You need to be real and know that most people seek out professionals with medical degrees when they want health-related answers. But you may have a specialty in which you are wonderfully qualified. One of my clients has been a successful veterinarian for twenty-five years. When she came to me, she wanted to speak about health and fitness for people. I knew her greatest strength would be to talk about what working with animals taught her about human health and wellness. She is eminently qualified to speak on that topic, and her speech is riveting.

How Others See You

When you get up in front of an audience, how you look takes on added significance. You are up in front, and everyone is looking at you. The rule here is "no distractions." It's important to wear clothing that flatters your body. Accentuate what you love about yourself, and camouflage the parts that aren't perfect. For example, I have never worn any skirts above the knee because I am very aware of knees. I have chubby ones. I deal with it! Here are some general rules:

1. Make sure your clothes fit right. Ladies, this means you should not wear blouses that pull at the buttons. My office manager's mom has a great phrase for this: "You're still a size large even if you can barely button the size medium." I say wear the larger size so that there are no distractions. Plus, you will be more comfortable. For men, the same thing applies. An ill-fitting suit is distracting to some members of your audience.

2. If you have nervous habits, work on minimizing them. See details in the chapter titled "Preparing to Conquer Your Nervousness." Here are some general tips to help you feel prepared and ready before you speak:

   - Take three deep, relaxing breaths prior to the meeting. Breathe in and out very slowly.

- Close your eyes and roll your head very slowly in deep circles from one shoulder to the back, to the other shoulder, to your chest. Repeat three times and then reverse direction.

- Lift your shoulders up as high as you can, hold for ten seconds, and drop them. Repeat.

- Tighten your fists. Keep them clenched for five seconds and then quickly open them.

- Yawn two or three really big, exaggerated yawns. Repeat.

- Exercise daily. It's generally good for relaxing tension.

3. Be honest. Be yourself.

4. Be true to your values. People are checking out your clothes, but you're still naked emotionally. Everything you feel and believe is on your face. You need to be aware of that. Always tell the exact truth. You are not writing a resume. Do not exaggerate even one tiny thing. I never compromise my values to get a customer. I require that you are able to do two things before you become my client. First, you know exactly what you are selling—your product or service. If you are confused, I will refer you to a life coach or business coach. Second, you need to be able to say, "I am good at what I do." I can't give you that core confidence.

5. Know your target market, and stick to it. You can't be all things to all people. The first speech I ever turned down was for a Christian conference. I instantly knew I could not do it because I am Jewish. I said to the client, very nicely, "You deserve a keynote speaker who embraces Christ as their Lord and Savior. I do not, so I'm not the right person." They were so grateful.

Develop Patience

It takes time to develop a new skill. Be patient. Patience is a lost art in our society. Today, when we talk about being patient, we want it in the other person. When I talk about patience, I mean tolerating delay—accepting it without complaint. I practiced this a lot on a speaking trip to Brazil, sitting in taxis snarled in traffic, and the point was driven home to me in a serendipitous way that afternoon at the spectacular Botanical Gardens in Rio. Lo and behold, here was the sign in front of the Orchid House:

"Sponsoring the Orchid House was the largest outcome of the admiration that jewelry artist Antonio Bernardo has for orchids," says the sign. "His dedication to these plants provided him with something else: patience. 'I wouldn't say I'm a patient person, but I have some patient aspects,' Bernardo writes. 'I exercise them when dealing with orchids and creating jewels. I'm capable of creating a jewel that must be welded 800 times. This takes patience, calm and control, as do plants.'"

How impressive is that? 800 times! Patience, calm, and control are characteristics vital to growing and sustaining our businesses and to developing your perfect marketing pitch. How do we cultivate these three virtues? One minute at a time. Here are the thoughts I keep top of mind to remind me to be patient. They may help you as well.

1. While working at Disney, I learned, "Everything is for my entertainment or my education, so if it's not fun, I must be learning." Or, as my sister says, "What's the blessing in this stressing?"

2. Be like an athlete: shake off the bad play—or the rejection from a potential client. Let it go. Don't carry it with you a moment more. Each moment is a new moment of now.

3. EGBOK. Everything's gonna be okay. Really.

Be Resilient

One of the characteristics you need when you embark on crafting and delivering a marketing speech is resilience. Many of you and I have bounced back from some of the worst business times in our lives. Just like sports teams, we demonstrate "worst to first": after a crummy year, we can end up having our best year ever. It's all about training yourself to be resilient, which is best defined as "the ability to recover quickly from misfortune; the capacity to withstand stress and catastrophe." We resilient people work with adversity in such a way that we come through unharmed or even better for the experience. It's the quality of character that allows a group of people, a work group, or sports team to rebound from misfortune, hardships, and traumas. There is a good deal of current research on people who are resilient.

Here are their core characteristics:

1. They have strong social support.

2. They value communicating with others.

3. They possess unshakable optimism (most important)—this is your ace in the hole.

4. They possess the capacity to recover, to get back up and get on with it.

When I coach entrepreneurs of a certain age, I often say the great thing about getting older is, "We know stuff, and don't doubt ourselves. We don't sweat the small stuff; we trust our ability to withstand any great stress; we bounce back; we are resilient!"

Chapter 4
Prepare About Your Purpose

"Speak only if it improves upon the silence."
– Gandhi

How do you persuade customers or clients? The only way you can get someone to give you what you want—to persuade them to use your product or service—is to leave no doubt in their minds. Be clear about what you want them to do.

What Are You Selling?

When I coach people to speak about their business, I urge them to analyze the audience. You have to be passionate about the needs, problems, and situations of the audience, but first you need to be passionate about *your* product or service. It's the solution for your customer's need, problem, or situation.

When you prepare a presentation, don't ask, "What do I want to tell the people?" Instead, ask yourself, "What is it that my audience needs to know? What do I want my audience to do, think, or feel after my presentation?" The next time you hear a speaker, you'll be able to tell whether they are telling you what they want to tell you or whether they have you in mind.

19

What if the presentation doesn't seem to motivate an action on the audience's part? Some people think they *just* give an update on their product or service. And whenever somebody says, "It's just a ...," a red flag goes up for me. You *just* give an update? What do you really want the audience to do, think, or feel after you speak? Do you want credibility?

Yes. Do you want continued support for what you're doing? Yes. You always want people to know you are credible, to support you, and to think you're fabulous.

Every presentation you give needs to motivate your audience to do, think, or feel something. Otherwise, why are you even speaking?

Chapter 5

Prepare About Your Audience

*"I know there is strength in the differences
between us. I know there is comfort,
where we overlap."*

– Ani DiFranco

The More You Know, the Better the Flow

The most important part of your speech preparation process is in *knowing* your audience. The better you know your audience, the better your words will flow. There's no magic potion here; analyzing your audience is hard work. Once you know who they are, you will be able to customize your presentation to their needs.

Audience Analysis

When you answer the following questions, you will have an audience profile upon which you can develop a sound presentation strategy. Here's an overview of the questions to follow:

- Who is in the audience?
- What are their attitudes and expectations?
- What is their level of jargon and technical expertise?

- What is their preferred way to receive information?
- What are their time tolerances?
- What is their level of interest in my subject?
- What is my credibility?
- What are their personal interests and hobbies?
- What are their "**hot buttons**"?

To help you effectively analyze your audience, I've created this easy to complete form that you can download here: http://www. pitchperfect.biz/

Will This Be on My Test?

Why do you need to analyze your audience? By knowing them, you can *motivate* them to buy your product or service. How do you do that?

Here's a little story I tell about motivating people. Once upon a time, when you were eight years old, you were sitting in a third-grade classroom listening to the teacher. The teacher was up in front, and he or she was droning on and on. It was *boring*, and you were falling asleep. Suddenly a little obnoxious child in the back row stands up and yells out, "Hey, teacher, is this going to be on the test?" And everybody is very embarrassed that he asked this question. You all avoided direct eye contact with the teacher. But you all listened very carefully to the answer because if the answer was, "No, this isn't going to be on the test. This is just something interesting I want you to know," what was your response? Yes, you stopped listening. You looked out the window. You put your pencil down. You leaned back, and you fell asleep. "Whew, it's not on the test."

But what if the response was, "Yes, this will be a very important part of the test." What was your response? You sat up straighter. "Could you repeat that? Can I borrow a pencil, please? What was that again?" You wrote it down. Because it was *ON THE TEST*! My perhaps cynical view of human beings is that ever since you were eight years old, you have been trying to figure out what's on "the test." And when you figure it out, or you think you have, you will do only the things that are *on your test.* And that's all.

I taught five-year-olds when I was getting my Master's. Five-year-olds don't have tests yet. It's their most wonderful quality. You can say, "Okay everybody, come join the circle." And they do. And you say, "Okay everybody, cross your arms and legs." And they do. They don't ask questions. They do it just for the sake of doing it. Now if I said to a roomful of adults, "Alright everybody, come join a circle," you would ask, "Why?" You would try to determine if this was on your test. You might look around. If the boss or a line starts coming up to the front, you would most likely follow. And as you came up, the women would tug at their tops, and the men would tuck in their shirts because no one wants to look shabby. That's a test item that begins in teenage years. "How long will this take?" is another specific test question. And the most important test question for adults is, "You're not going to make me do anything dumb, are you?" because no one wants to be singled out or look foolish. All of these examples are qualifying questions to find out if this is *on your test.*

Your employees and your teenagers and all the people you manage in your life are always asking, "Is this on my test?" And in order to get your priorities done, in order to motivate people, what do you have to do? You need to put your priority items on their test. People have a whole stack of priorities they want to get done, and yours is only one of them. Your job is to get yourself from the bottom of their pile to the top. So you add your priority item to their test.

Here's the rub. People are individuals, and they have individual tests. And *you* have to figure out what to put on their test.

The first consideration in developing an effective presentation is to accurately assess your audience by finding out what's on their test—what's important to them. There are a number of sources who can provide you with information about the problems, needs, biases, and attitudes of your audience. Some of these are people who will be attending your speech, prior speakers, and the person who invited you to speak. Perhaps you can interview some key listeners or check out the group on the Internet.

Take the time to do a thorough audience analysis and remember:

Mimi says...

"Don't be afraid to ask dumb questions. They're easier to handle than dumb mistakes."

Tailoring Your Speech to Gender Differences

Do you change your speech depending on the gender of the audience? Perhaps a bit but not radically. There *are* differences in the way women and men listen. Because of early social pressure to be "good girls" and "little ladies," women get the message that being confrontational isn't acceptable. Often women hear their inner voice say, "Speak up," but many squelch these messages because of upbringing and the early lessons about being quiet or courteous. Women have been socialized to avoid verbal confrontation more than men, and to speak more politely.

It's important to consider some of the basic differences between men and women. Even if you think you personally don't fit the typical mold for your gender, it's guaranteed that you will speak to men and women who do.

The following sections contain four strategies for women who want to get their message across to men. If you practice one of these strategies each week, you'll quickly alter the way others perceive you. The prerequisite is to start listening to yourself. Awareness is the first step to any behavioral change. Accept and grow, or be left in the dust in the world of communicating.

Four Strategies for Women Who Want Men to Hear Their Message

Strategy #1: Avoid apologies

Women tend to be more apologetic than men. Even assertive women sometimes unwittingly use power-robbing devices in their speech. If you have something to say, don't apologize for saying it, and don't lose your impact with generalities or vague references. Here are the specific devices under the general banner of apologies:

Prefacing and tagging

Prefacing and *tagging* refer to those little extra words before and after a statement:

- Prefacing: leading into a statement with a phrase that weakens it. For example, "I'm not sure about this, but ...."

- Tagging: adding a qualifying phrase at the end of a statement. For example, "We should take action, don't you think?" "Don't you think" or "Isn't that right" are typical tags.

Questioning tone

A *questioning tone* is intonation that goes up at the end of a sentence. This takes the power right out of an otherwise declarative sentence. To the listener, the speaker sounds as if she is unsure and lacks self-confidence. What the tone communicates is, "Don't you agree?" Or worse: "Please agree quickly so that I know that what I just said has value." Listen for upward intonation when some women introduce themselves and what they do for a living.

If you don't have confidence in what you say, how can you expect anybody else to have faith in you? Listen to yourself or ask a trusted friend. If you find that you have this power-reducing habit, start practicing today to get rid of it. Remember, awareness is the first step to behavioral change, and you are now aware.

Hedges or qualifiers

Women tend to use many little words like "kind of" and "sort of" that rob their statements of power. If you use these phrases, it is a habit. You can break this habit and bring more power into your speech right now. A few examples are:

- "I kind of think that ...."
- "We probably should really ...."
- "It seems like a fairly good way to ...."
- "Kind of/sort of ..." or "It's sort of like ...."

26

- "You maybe need to …."

These phrases don't just contain extra words, they contain *unsure* words. Using these weak words can make *you* appear weak.

Perhaps you developed these speech patterns to cover your rear end. They are risk-avoiding phrases that may indicate you're reluctant to state issues definitively. Beware of sounding indecisive or hesitant when you want to convey certainty. You don't need to banish these words from your repertoire. You can use them when you desire to hedge your bets. The point is to be able to choose whatever words you need to achieve your goals.

Non-words and non-phrases

Non-words are the extras that get plugged into speech—words or syllables that take the place of silence by giving you a pause to pull together your next thought. Non-words show up in the darnedest places, and they always slow up or divert an otherwise fine presentation.

Here are just a few examples:
- "Really": as in, "Really, I really want to go forward."
- "Like": as in, "Do you want to go, like, forward?"
- "Um": as in, "um," or "uh."

Use silence to give power to your statement and opinions. Practice the power of the pause in your very next presentation.

Strategy #2: Be brief

For women, talk is connection. Women talk to build a relationship. Men use talk to exchange information.

Women generally use more details in their conversation than men. The information you want the male listener to hear may be lost in all those details. Watch for signs that a male listener is glazing over, and cut down on the number of words immediately. Men feel they are responsible for the energy they allot to a certain activity. Some feel the need to "set their energy clocks" so that they don't run out of energy. Running out of energy makes men feel out of control—a feeling they hate.

Men don't use a lot of words. For many years, while on breaks from my training courses, I've been observing men going to lunch. One guy turns to the other and says, "Lunch?" The other guy says, "Sure." That's it. They don't say, "Wanna go to lunch?" "Yeah, it sounds like a great idea. Where shall we go?" "I don't know. Where shall we go?" No. It's just, "Lunch?" "Sure." To men, that is a conversation.

This pattern starts in childhood. My friend has a son and a daughter. They returned from their first day in school, and their mom asked each of them how their first day of school went. The little boy said, "Fine. Can I go play ball?" The little girl said, "Well, I got on the bus and there was Suzie, so I sat next to her and ... and then ... and then ...." She took fifteen minutes to answer the question.

The children were each communicating in their own gender-based style, which comes naturally. Studies show that women use an average of 25,000 words in a typical day. Men use about 15,000 words in the same day. I always quip, "The problem is that by the time men come home from work, they've used all 15,000 up. We haven't even started on our 25,000. We've had to be concise all day long!"

My boyfriend used to hang on every word of my stories. Then we got serious. I started a story, and he stopped me, saying, "Meem, wait. Are you going to do, 'he said-she said/he said-she said'?" That was his code for the way I tell stories from the beginning with all the details, chronologically to the end. (Men are wincing just reading this.)

And I remember my response, "Tsk (sigh)." Men hate that response because it's a sneaky way of saying, "You stupid idiot," without actually saying it.

I said, "Tsk (sigh), yes, honey. That's how the story is enjoyed the best."

And he said, "Not by me. Can you just skip to the bottom line?"

I remember feeling offended—I thought he was going to miss the good part. Then I discovered that the story is not the good part for him. He really did want the bottom line. Men seem to be more about the destination than the journey. Women are all about the journey.

When I put a moratorium on my storytelling, my boyfriend had to *beg* me to tell him the whole story. And he had to promise to listen *all* the way through, without the head-rolling gesture. Women hate that gesture because it's a sneaky, nonassertive, passive-aggressive way of saying, "Hurry up!" without actually saying it. It's the male version of "Tsk (sigh)," and if they use it too often, I know plenty of women who will use an alternate hand gesture.

Strategy #3: Be direct—don't hint

In addition to brevity, men desire clear messages. Do them a favor: be direct. Here's a story from my "men and women" speech.

Men and women have different attitudes about hinting. Men don't like hints. A woman may give a man big hints over and over, such as, "I love flowers." And no flowers arrive. So she gives him *huge* hints next, such as (upon seeing a person delivering flowers to a door) saying to him, "Oh look. I love flowers." She waits and no flowers arrive. Finally, she decides to be direct: "Honey," she says one day, "Do you know what I would really love you to do?"

He looks up attentively. This is a focusing statement. It gives him *hope* that the next thing out of her mouth will be specific. "What?" he asks.

She says, "I would love you to bring me flowers sometime, when I least expect it, like on my birthday."

He gets the message. She can tell! It clicks. She gets gorgeous flowers on her birthday. She is so happy. Her women friends are livid. "You had to *tell* him," they say. "It's not romantic," they say. "He should have known," they say.

"Right!" she answers back. "On the one hand, I could have said, 'He should have known.' On the other hand, I could have *flowers*. I went for the flowers, and I'm so glad I did."

When she debriefs him on this incident, she may say, "What were you thinking for two years when I said, 'I love flowers'?" And he loves that question; it's analytical. He says, "I remember I had a warm feeling because it's so feminine, and I also thought you should probably plant some."

"I love flowers" means "I love flowers" to men. They don't search for hidden meanings. They listen literally.

Men wrote the dictionary. They are literal. Men usually say what they mean and mean what they say.

Strategy #4: Avoid emotional displays

Men have been socialized to be less emotionally demonstrative. As a result, crying or other emotional displays in a presentation can be more distracting than a low-cut dress. Women have not been socialized in the same way as men. In fact, women cry four times more frequently than men, according to a Minnesota-based study.

The crying person seems to manipulate a sympathetic response from the listener. Crying also annoys and angers people who have shut off their own feelings. If they don't want to deal with their own feelings, they don't want to deal with anyone else's. Audiences may feel that a woman who cries is being manipulative.

The good news is your purpose is not to evoke sad feelings; it's to celebrate what you have to offer and how potential clients can benefit from your expertise.

Four Strategies for Men Who Want Women to Hear What They Have to Say

Some speech mannerisms, common among men, are so off-putting to women that they rob men of the opportunity to be heard no matter how valuable the words are. This concept is not just theory. Because women have become a major force in the workplace, men will benefit by altering their style to communicate successfully with women.

The following sections contain four strategies for men who want women to hear what they have to say. The prerequisite is to start listening to yourself. Again, awareness is the first step to any behavioral change.

This isn't right or wrong—it's simply true.

Strategy #1: Don't be condescending with "honey," "baby," "sweetie."

It's the 21ˢᵗ century! That any American male can still be using words like "honey," "sweetie," and "baby" to address a woman in the workplace is shocking. For a man to use these phrases in a presentation—even when quoting himself—is entirely inappropriate. When your words flow from a place of respect, you don't have to worry about compromising your credibility.

Strategy #2: Share before deciding

Sharing does not come naturally to most men. They have been socialized in the "strong, silent" stereotype. They must have things all figured out before they say anything about a subject.

When you are speaking, the audience wants to know your process, so share it—especially with a mostly female audience. Instead of coming across as lacking, you'll be perceived as honest and confident.

Strategy #3: Share something personal

This is not a suggestion to be intrusive or sexual. This approach is essentially humanizing. Joseph Campbell reminds us about the importance of story in our lives. Even though this approach may not seem natural for you at first, share stories of humankind with your audience. Illustrate a family story. Provide some of the detail. Most women love details.

Men are better off making personal comments about their own lives, not about a woman's personal life or appearance. Because of the history of sexual harassment in this country, men do not have the same freedom that a woman has to comment on the clothing or appearance of the opposite sex.

It's not fair, but it's true. If a man thinks a dress is attractive, he should keep that to himself. If he likes an item that is personal but not quite as personal as a dress, and it's part of the story, he can go ahead and comment on it. The smart advice is, "When in doubt, don't."

Strategy #4: Avoid emotional displays

Yelling and other emotional displays can be just as ruinous to a man's position as crying can be for a woman. Men have been socialized to be less demonstrative with all their emotions except anger. Many men still think yelling when they are frustrated or angry is acceptable behavior. In fact, men yell much more frequently than women in the office, according to a recent study.

The man who raises his voice signals to the listeners and observers that—for the moment at least—this individual is incapable of handling a situation. Yelling also creates shame and resentment in those subjected to the outburst. If they are not able to yell back, they may get even in other ways. Not only do women feel that a man who raises his voice is being dominating and controlling, but other men may question his level of confidence.

Women and men can learn from each other. Respect the differences and alter your style so that you can be heard. Remember: you can think you are the world's best communicator, but if your words are not heard, your message doesn't matter.

What's your style—formal or casual?

Not all differences are gender-based; some of them have to do with personal style. There are those of us who have a "formal" relationship with *time*; I am one. If I'm not twenty minutes early, I feel late. I fret if I *think* I will be late, and I create "impending disaster" scenarios that all begin with "what if ...." I'm also formal with physical things as well. In my home and office I know where everything is because there's a place for everything and everything is in its place. If it's not there, it must be *stolen*.

Some people have a "casual" relationship with time. They're the one ones who say I'll be there "about" ten o'clock instead of "at" ten o'clock. It's just a different style of being in the world. These differences between time and things are what made *The Odd Couple* such an incredible success. The "formal" people were relating to Felix while the "casual" people were totally in synch with Oscar.

Those with a "casual" relationship with time and things tell us to "chill." They leave *much* later than we would for the airport, and traffic seems to *clear out* for them. No disasters occur, and they arrive *just* on time, much to our dismay. Our dismay, partly, is nervousness for them that something might happen, but the big reason we formal people are dismayed is that they get there *on time* (from their point of view), and they didn't *seem* to have any stress about it.

It's the same story with their casual relationship with things. Nothing is ever "lost." In fact, they may resent formal types for labeling an item "lost." *They* say it's *misplaced* and it will *show up*. And they don't seem to worry about it.

It's smart to keep these differences in mind when writing and delivering your presentation for your audience.

Chapter 6
Preparing to Conquer Your Nervousness
Is There Any Hope?

"Hope is the feeling you have that the feeling you have isn't permanent."

– Jean Kerr

You will have many opportunities to speak in front of groups of people if that's what you want. Maybe you are often called on to speak at meetings, even if it's only a few people. And the more responsibility you have on the job, or as a business owner, the more opportunities you will have to speak up. Real communication takes place when the speaker connects with a person or group on both a rational and an emotional level. The communication is cemented when the listener is completely involved with the speaker's message. The connection can be broken in one of two ways: first, when the message (content) is wrong and the listener tunes out; the second, more familiar way the connection can be broken is when the speaker's nervousness shows in ways that are distracting to the listener.

How Do I Stop Being Nervous?

Everybody is worried about "stage fright," but nervousness is simply energy gone wrong. The body produces energy, which is normal and good. We get into trouble as presenters when we try to squelch or deny our energy. When we try to squelch our energy, it still comes out, but it manifests as nervousness—knocking knees, dry mouth, sweaty hands, and more. People have told me that their knees knocked, but I didn't believe it until I actually saw a man's trousers start to quiver right at knee level. I could see his pants move, so I knew the guy was shaking. Instead of suppressing your energy/nervousness, release it. You need to think of your energy as coming up and out of your body, releasing, and giving it away. The energy behind your message comes up and out through the five channels of the body: your eyes, hands, feet, body, and voice.

Here's a little story about energy. You're walking through a dark, deep forest (think Hansel and Gretel). It's the middle of the night, and there's not a sound except the crunching of the leaves under your feet. Suddenly, you feel the ground reverberating behind you. The footsteps come closer and closer, and pretty soon they're right behind you. You feel hot breath on your neck, maybe a drop of saliva. Slowly you turn, and there behind you is a seven-foot-tall grizzly bear, tongue hanging out, looking hungry. What do you do? (Actually, the right answer is fall down and play dead. If you are a bear expert, you know that.)

But for the purpose of my example, what you fear is not a bear. It's your ego. What can you do to escape it? Turn around and run like heck! That's the flight response. It may save your life (or your speech). You must channel your energy up and out through the five channels. You're looking out through your eyes (hopefully you haven't closed them), and they show you where to go. You're channeling energy through your feet, hopefully propelling you forward. Your arms are propelling you forward. Your voice may be screaming to give you extra energy to go forward. Your body is hopefully leaning that way. So these channels are working to save your life.

What's another choice that you could make if there were a bear behind you? Freeze. If, instead of channeling the energy up and out to save your life, you suppressed your energy and froze, you could get eaten. A dangerous situation like the bear in the forest is exactly like the dangerous situation of your being in front of an audience. *The Book of Lists* cites public speaking as the number one fear people have. Death is number five. So when you say, "I'd rather die than speak in public," it has the ring of truth. Almost everyone experiences some degree of nervousness when they have to be a speaker, whether it's a formal speech in front of a group, presenting a proposal to a decision maker, or being called on in a meeting to answer a question. You feel your heart pounding, your throat constricting, your face feeling hot, and your mouth drying up. For some people this feeling will never go away completely. You may never truly banish the butterflies; the best you can do is persuade them to fly in formation.

Two Things Audiences Won't Forgive

The truth is audiences really *want* you to succeed. There are very few things they can't forgive. They want you to make it. If your voice cracks, it's fine. I know of only two things audiences won't forgive: being phony and making them nervous. (Actually, these are two of the things in *life* that people won't forgive you for.) "Be authentic," the experts say. Indeed, authenticity seems to be the value of the moment. The dictionary defines "authentic" as "real" or "genuine." In an age of online social networking and dating, people are creating digital versions of themselves, and being yourself seems to be the best way to sell yourself. So when you get up to present your business in front of an audience, resist the impulse to become a "speaker"; that is, using a voice more formal than your own and taking dramatic pauses. These are dead giveaways of phoniness. Being real in front of an audience of any size is the best way to grow your business.

The next few sections detail how to transform your nervousness into positive energy through the five channels of your body.

The Five Channels of Energy

"Nothing great was ever achieved without enthusiasm."

– Ralph Waldo Emerson

Let's look at the five channels of energy and at how we can channel our energy up and out through those five channels.

Channel #1 – The Eyes

The first channel is the eyes. Your eyes are the most important way to give away your energy. If I came up to you and said, without looking you in the eye, "I really think you're going to like my program; it will help you grow your business," would you believe me? Why not? Because I wasn't looking at you. People don't believe you when you're not looking into their eyes. Everything you've learned about making eye contact is true. Some teachers tell you that when you speak, look above everybody's head to a point far away. I say no. I believe you should focus on a person, one person per thought. Focus on one person, finish the thought. Turn to another person in another part of the room to make another point. Make sure you include everyone in the whole room. Some of the conference rooms you speak in will have long tables, and you may be in the middle of the table. You have people on one side and people on the other side, and you're constantly looking from side to side. Make sure that you spend at least five beats per side—the time of one whole thought. Focus on this side, then switch over and focus on someone else. Be inclusive.

Eye-to-Eye Contact

Eye-to-eye contact conveys credibility, sincerity, involvement, and interest in your message and your audience. People believe you. They also believe you're interested in your message. If you're not looking at them, people think you're not interested, or that what you're saying is not interesting. So giving out energy through eye contact is the most important of the five channels. The next time you watch a speaker, note the quality of their eye contact. Some will focus on the ceiling or the floor or flit their eyes quickly. How does that make them look? Unsure or nervous? You want to stay focused and make eye contact. One person at a time. One thought at a time.

Who Should You Look At?

I say, practice *selective hooking*. I know that sounds a little risqué. What I mean is select the individuals in the audience who are nodding and smiling at you, and *hook* them with your eye contact. No matter how stiff and cold you think your audience may be, there's going to be somebody out there feeling for you, wanting you to make it, or knowing how you feel because they too have stood before audiences, trying their best.

Practice at Home

Practice at home using pillows, parts of furniture, or pieces of paper with cartoon faces drawn on them and then taped to chairs as your audience. Talk to them. Linger on each for about five seconds or the length of a thought or phrase. Get help from a child, friend, or spouse if you feel the need for feedback.

Channel #2 – Hands

Your hands are the second presentation element. Don't try to plan what to do with your hands. They will move naturally if and when you're giving out enough energy through your eyes and voice. If your voice is a low monotone and your eyes are downcast, your hands are simply not motivated to move. When hand energy is suppressed, it comes out as fidgeting. People wring their hands, steeple their fingers, and fold their hands in front of their body like a fig leaf. Men typically slide their hands into their pockets or hide them behind their backs. I make them stop, even though some have told me, "I need it to relax." I tell them, "The audience doesn't care about you. They care about *themselves.*" Women put their hands in their pockets too, but their pockets are usually so tight that when they attempt to gesture, you can see the little fingernails sticking out from the pockets. And that is distracting! Pointing at the audience makes people feel accused or put on the spot. Don't do that. Anything you do below your waist is very distracting. You don't want listeners' eyes focused anywhere but on your face. That's where your power and sincerity come from.

So the rule is: don't do anything distracting! You know the old joke. You go to the doctor knowing you'll be billed big bucks for this visit. You say, "Oh doctor, it hurts when I do this!" and the doctor says, "Then don't do that." I agree. Don't do anything that is distracting.

Let your words and genuine desire to connect drive your gestures.

Laser Pointer

What if you want to use a laser pointer? Think again. I've never seen anybody use it well. You have to be very experienced to use one. Often, speakers use the pointer to highlight something on a slide and their hand shakes, which makes the light shake. Then they forget the pointer is in their hand. They may be so nervous that they use the pointer to gesture because they forget they have it, and audience members try to follow the beam. The result? Distraction!

Support Your Message

Use your hands to support your message. You use your hands to count, indicate size, show spatial relationships, show movement, and emphasize points. Keep them above your waist as much as possible. When you start a presentation, keep them down at your sides. When the energy in your eye contact and your voice is enough to send energy to your hands, they will move naturally. You don't have to worry about them. If your hands don't come alive, it means you're using a monotone, you're not making eye contact, or you're not impassioned about your speaking. Ratchet up your energy, and make the magic happen.

Fake It

Now, how do you get impassioned about your subject when your subject is not something you're passionate about? You've heard the phrase, "Fake it till you make it." Be the most emphatic person in the room. Professionals are people who get the job done even when they don't feel like it. So if you don't feel like it, or it's just not an interesting topic, *fake it*! When you fake it, you will indeed make it. You will get energized.

Practice at Home

Pick a topic and talk about it looking at yourself in the mirror. Expand the use of your hands for gestures. Notice the size of the area in which you can comfortably use your hands for gestures and still maintain your professional image.

Channel #3 – Feet

Another channel of energy is your feet. Balance your weight evenly on both feet like an athlete with your knees flexed. Remember the bear in the forest—you need to be ready to *go*! You don't want to be sitting back on your heels or locking your joints. It takes valuable seconds to lean forward and start to move. You want to be balanced on the soles of your feet so that you're ready to take a step.

Some people aimlessly pace. That distracts the audience; people start anticipating your actions. Other speakers are planted like trees, and the suppressed energy can make them sway. That's the sign of an amateur. If you want to take a couple steps, make sure what you are saying motivates you to do it. Make your movements purposeful. Walk forward a couple steps only if you feel passionate about a point you're making.

I "paper train" some of my clients who wander aimlessly about. They get a piece of 8 ½ by 11-inch paper (with footprints) to stand on, and they can't move off it. Rather than stepping off the paper, I encourage them to channel the nervous energy that makes them want to pace, to channel that energy into powering their voice and establishing energetic eye contact.

Channel #4 – Body

And then there's posture. You don't want to hunch over and look nervous. You want to have energy in your body. Like everything else, you don't want your body to be distracting.

Check It Out

Look at yourself in the mirror before you speak. Notice how far apart your feet are. The "at-ease" position may be comfortable for the speaker, but it's distracting to the audience. They want to see legs positioned almost together. Remember, the audience doesn't care about you and what makes you less nervous. They only care that you don't make them nervous.

Shifting Hips

Watch the shifting of hips. Men do shifting hips by putting weight on one foot and then the other. They get sort of rhythmical about it. The audience is listening, but they're thinking, "Oh there he goes. ... Oh, there he went." Women do something else. If they wear heels that are too high and uncomfortable, they plant a heel on the floor and lift their toes to rest for a moment. If the woman gets nervous and energy starts flowing, she might start "drilling for oil" with that heel, which *really* distracts the audience. And then she shifts and drills on the other side. The way to end all that nervous stuff is to make sure you're giving out energy through your voice and eyes. Walk forward only when you are motivated—when you're impassioned—and make your movements purposeful.

What You're Wearing

Clothes shouldn't be distracting. Make sure they fit. Have someone check you over before you speak. You can't see if your collar is turned up in back, but some nitpicker in your audience will.

Channel #5 – Voice

The fifth channel of energy is your voice. Your voice expresses and emphasizes your message. No one likes to listen to the drone of a monotone speaker. You need to project your voice. Vocal characteristics can make or break your presentation.

Five Vocal Characteristics

1. Pace. Some people get paid to talk really fast in commercials on television, but you can't do that. You have to talk at a speed the audience can understand. There are people ... who talk so ... slowly ... that you just want to shake them. Too slow is a no-no; the audience gets bored. Make sure your pace is right for the listening audience. The only way to do that is to tape your speech and listen to yourself, painful as it may be. Or ask a friend: "Do I speak too fast or too slowly?"

Varying the tempo adds quality to any presentation. Speeding up or slowing down at appropriate, natural intervals to emphasize certain points will focus attention on your message. It helps the audience easily identify the concepts you consider important. The underlying concept used to make tempo effective is contrast. Contrast between tempos (fast and slow, serious and light, loud and soft), when done to emphasize concepts, can also enhance your persuasiveness. When explaining something that requires energy and force, speed to a natural crescendo. For an important point, follow with a slower-paced delivery to hold the audience's attention.

2. Intonation. Intonation is the variety in the voice, the ups and downs. The opposite of good intonation is monotone. Sometimes, when presenters are given technical material to talk about, they lapse into monotone. I used to think of it as the "aerospace monotone" because that's where I first heard it. But no, it's present in many companies and public sector institutions as well. People think they have to sound official. If your goal is to put your audience to sleep, use this technique. Otherwise avoid it like the plague.

Since you always want to have the beginning of your speech memorized, you can plan variety in your first two sentences. Write out the sentences and underline the important words, the ones you should really emphasize. When you look at those underlined words, you will naturally read them with more energy, and your voice will do what comes naturally.

3. Tone. Tone refers to the changing pitch of your voice and alters the meaning of words through varying inflections and emphasis. Depending on the emotion with which a speaker delivers a word, that speaker may give the word a new meaning. Tone is different from intonation. Tone is the attitude or emotion in your voice. It can be condescending, angry, sarcastic, impatient, or unsure. While we don't always realize it, our tone of voice can give us away. We might think we sound nice, but we have a not-nice tone in our voice. We can say the exact same phrases with two totally different tones. "I've told you before" can sound angry, accusing, or neutral, depending on your tone. Just as you check your collar to make sure it's right, make sure your emotions are clear and clean before you get up to speak.

4. Volume. Volume involves the louds and softs. You need to speak so that the person in the back of the room can hear you easily. Don't worry if your voice cracks. Audiences don't mind. They want you to be natural; they don't want you to be phony. Don't worry about correcting your voice. Don't worry about breathing. Just remember to speak clearly. If they can't hear you, they may turn to the person next to them, and ask, "What did she say?" and you may lose them. Don't mumble. It may make you appear incompetent. We have all suffered through a speaker who provided good information but whose lack of volume put the group to sleep. Volume adds a quality to language that not only stimulates attention, it also highlights words and clarifies meanings. To add energy and dynamics to your delivery, decide which points need emphasis, and color them by raising and lowering volume. This variation helps the audience know what to consider beneficial or important. Continual loud delivery is no better than constant whispering. You don't want your audience to go away feeling either left out or battered.

5. Non-words and non-phrases (e.g., "um, like, really, you know, okay"). You may be acquainted with people who end every sentence with "okay." You might want to say, "No, it's not okay." Non-words create noise, not meaning. Some people are totally unaware of their speech patterns. Start listening to yourself to determine if you have a non-word habit. Some people use them so that they don't have to face the risk of silence. You've all heard of the "power of the pause." It's true. It's very powerful to allow some silences to occur. Trust the silences. They create interest and add impact to what you're saying. Own the space in the room so that you can feel secure being silent. If you forget where you are in your presentation, don't be afraid of pausing, but avoid saying "um." That's amateurish. Look for some friendly face, and make eye contact until you remember what you were talking about.

Practice at Home

- Read aloud ten minutes daily—the paper, poetry, or a magazine article. Get used to hearing your own voice. Practice being more expressive. Use lots of intonation and vary your phrasing.

- Read a passage of about 400 to 420 words into a digital recorder. Play it back and notice the time it takes to read the passage. If it takes much more than three minutes or considerably less than three minutes, read it again, changing your pace. It should take about three minutes.

- If you don't project well, read part of an article into a digital recorder for about one minute. Listen to it. Then do the same passage again at a higher projection and volume level. Listen to yourself again. Notice how you physically feel in your throat, your head, your mouth, and your breathing when you are at the better volume and projection levels. Aim to replicate those physical feelings in your pitch. With practice you will improve.

Six Tips to Combat Nervousness

The point is *everybody* gets nervous, even Johnny Carson during his entire thirty years of doing monologues. Johnny famously admitted that he got totally crazy nervous before he went on for his opening monologue. He couldn't eat; his palms would sweat. He would get shivers and colds and shakes and hots. But did you know it watching him on television? No. What he did was he made his energy work *for* him, not *against* him. He gave it away through his eyes, hands, feet, body, and voice, and he never looked nervous. That's the secret. Increase your energy to overcome nervousness. It's the only way.

Here are six tips that I use even after more than thirty years of professional speaking:

1. Be prepared. Nothing makes you more confident than having a well-worded, humorous speech. (You may need a speech coach. The good news? I am close at hand.)

2. Drink water. Stay hydrated to avoid cotton mouth. Have a glass of room temperature water close by. Take a drink after you give your audience something to think about. Pet peeve: Don't pull from a water bottle in front of an audience. You're not at the gym!

3. Exercise to get the excess energy out of the way. Many male readers will remember my presentation skills classes where I made them "drop and give me ten" push-ups before it was their turn to speak.

4. Embrace the endorphins. Nervousness is just energy gone wrong. Focus the energy out through your five channels, and you won't look nervous.

5. Visualizing is a technique frequently used by athletes and all sorts of performers to be successful. Instead of worrying about your presentation, actually imagine or *see* yourself successfully presenting. Focus on your audience and message instead of your butterflies. Move through this successful vision slowly. Visualize your audience nodding approvingly. Your brain accepts this act of imagining and begins to drive your actual behavior. Visualizing can create the win you want for yourself.

6. Before you speak, listen to or replay in your mind a rousing song that gets your juices flowing and gets you out of your head. I did this just the other day. I was on my way to Orange County to speak to 150 women, and I hit some heavy traffic. I like being **really** early, and it looked like this was not going to happen. I could feel my heart speed up, and I got the tingles, the pre-sweat condition in my body. So I turned on "Don't Stop Believin'" by Journey, volume all the way up, and started beating my imaginary drum with my right hand and singing at the top of my lungs: "IT GOES ON AND ON AND ON AND ON!" Another favorite: Bon Jovi's "Livin' on a Prayer" (I dare you to resist screaming to the chorus). One more: "More Than a Feeling" by Boston. The lyrics tell you what to do: "When I'm tired and thinkin' cold, I hide in my music, forget the day."

You get the point. Choose what works best for you, capture the feeling, and take it with you to your speech.

Chapter 7
Prepare to Organize Your Speech

*"Where observation is concerned, chance
favors only the prepared mind."*

– Louis Pasteur

Internalize one of Mimi's Laws of Great Speaking: "Never make an audience nervous." It's not just that the audience is reminded of eighth grade speech class; it's that they are way more sophisticated now. With the advent of TED Talks, people are used to well-structured excellence from the speaker on stage. They expect you to be smart and prepared, so definitely never, ever think you can "wing it."

Be Smart

Regarding being smart, I always say, "When you are presenting your product or service, you need to know 100 times more material about your subject than you actually will say in your speech." Here's why: the speech is just the skeleton of the subject on which you are an expert. It's the juicy high points of the company you own or book you wrote—or will write. You can't put *everything* you know into the speech. When a client insists, "We've gotta put this part in the speech! It's so good!" I say, "It is good, and it's good for your book—not the speech." Sometimes, I actually get a manila file folder, wave it in front of the client, and say, "We're going to put all this good stuff into your book!" And then I take their notes, put them into the file folder, and label it "The Book." Part of this is discipline, and part of it is that audiences don't expect a speech to be dense in content. They don't want to translate or figure out what you are saying. Remember, a speech is not written on a printed page. The audience can't look back to see what you were talking about. A speech is linear and temporal. It is said, and then it is gone. That's why you can't "wing it" when you are speaking.

Your speech needs to be organized. It needs to answer the questions in the listeners' brains as they arise so that the listeners are with you every step of the way.

Be Prepared

When you "wing it" (when you think you know your content so well you can just talk about it), you are trusting your brain to think in a linear fashion. Not so fast, my friend! What if it doesn't? What happens when you draw a blank? Do you root around in your notes right in front of the audience, muttering, "It's here somewhere ...," while the audience thinks, "Don't waste my time with your disorganization! Life is hard enough. I don't want to watch you struggle!"

Instead of winging it, follow these steps:

1. Use the Presentation Formula. Here's why: You want your audience to be with you the whole way. You want to avoid audience whiplash—you don't want the audience whipping their heads around to their neighbor and asking, "What did she say?" You want to look into the audience throughout your presentation and see nodding heads. If anyone is going to challenge you, you can see it. If you see frowns, address the objection. If you do this, all that's left for audience members to do is buy your product or service because you've answered all their objections.

2. Memorize your opening remarks very well. I say, "Lead with their need." You will prepare an opening that points out your audience's pain, need, or situation so that they are eager for the solutions your product or service provides. When they are engaged, they will lean in and listen. They are ready to learn and be entertained.

3. Learn your speech in "thought groups" or snippets, in stories or vignettes, not word for word. Point ... story ... repeat point. The story anchors the point. It's proof your point works. When you memorize your speech word for word, missing one word can trip you up. Horrors! Our brain remembers stories. This makes following notes much easier; you have bullet points, not pages of text that can be impossible to follow.

4. Have a great ending with a "call to action." People need to know what to do next to engage your services. Rehearse your ending so that it's smooth. Most importantly, be passionate about it. Exude lots of energy! Leave that energy with your audience so that they take a piece of you home with them.

All of this is made clear in part two of this book, "Engage Your Audience with Your Speech."

Part 2
Engage Your Audience with Your Speech

"Words form the thread on which we string our experiences."

– Aldous Huxley

Chapter 8

Starting to Write Your Speech

You have done all the hard work. Now, the fun begins.

- You have fleshed out your purpose—the exact product or service you are selling.

- You have examined your credentials and qualifications that make you uniquely qualified to sell what you're selling.

- You have analyzed your audience so that you can tailor your presentation to them and their style of listening.

- You have learned how to channel your nervousness into positive energy.

Now that you've learned how to channel your nervous energy, you're ready to make your content organized, relevant, and purposeful.

People will forgive you if you don't use your hands for gestures or if you shift your body weight unnecessarily, but they won't forgive you if you appear unprepared. When you waste someone's time, you insult them and do a disservice to yourself. (If you've ever sat through a presentation when this happened, you know how it felt.)

Now What?

Do you need to be talented? No. Do you need to have a huge personality?   Not necessarily.   You do need to have content that works, and that content needs to be positioned to address the audience's questions as they arise. You see, what makes a presentation effective is the positioning of the information.

Position Your Information

The tragedy sometimes is that people do prepare, but they do it so poorly the net impression is negative. What does "unprepared" look like?

- The "rambler," who never seems to make their point, bores the audience.
- The "skipper," whose thoughts don't flow logically one to the next, gives the audience whiplash.
- The "all about me" person spends too much time on their own "story," bores the audience.
- The "clueless" person speaks above or below the level of his/ her audience, the audience stops paying attention.

Pretend I have a glass of water and the water is information (content). I can either hand you the water (information) gracefully, or I can throw it in your face. Either way, you are going to get the content. When you hand information to your listeners slowly, they reach out to meet you halfway and take the information. That's why you position your content in a certain order. You answer the questions that appear in their minds—as they appear.

The presentation formula will help you present your ideas and effectively position your information. It follows the listener's frame of reference so that you can answer each question as it appears in the listener's mind.

You can download it here: http://www.pitchperfect.biz/

Here is the suggested timeline for a fifteen-minute speech:

Stages of a Presentation
15-minute Speech

Opening or Attention Getter

Brief; 30-60 seconds

Current Situation/Need/Problem

Brief; 30-45 seconds

Solution
General overview/recommendation;
2-3 minutes

Why You

1-2 minutes

Support/Proof
Major portion of the talk; Data/facts/rationale
5 minutes → infinite hours

"Why" Story
How you know this on a deeper level;
2 minutes

Call to Action
Specific, time related; 1 minute

Here is your worksheet:

Entrepreneur Speech Formula

Step 1. Open with their problem. **(Audience is thinking: "Why should I listen?")**

"How many of you [INSERT A PROBLEM THE AUDIENCE HAS]?"

_____

_____

_____

_____

_____

_____

Step 2. Briefly promise them how you will solve their problem. **(Audience is thinking: "So you're going to help me solve my problem? HOW?")**

"Today, I'm going to show you [HOW MY PRODUCT/ SERVICE CAN SOLVE YOUR PROBLEM]."

_____

_____

_____

_____

_____

_____

Step 3. Prove to them you're an expert. Offer your credibility. **(Audience is thinking: "Okay, why are YOU the one I should listen to?")**

"I know this because [INSERT YOUR EXPERTISE]."

_____

_____

_____

_____

_____

Step 4. Show them the way with features and benefits. **(Audience is thinking: "Well, what do you mean? Give me a taste of what to do to solve my problem, to alleviate my pain.")**

"Here's a taste of [HOW MY PRODUCT/SERVICE CAN HELP SOLVE YOUR PROBLEM]."

You may want to include:

- Example
- Statistic
- Testimony / Authority
- Analogy
- Fact

_____

_____

_____

_____

_____

_____

Step 5. Include more proof. **(Audience is thinking: "That's good. Give me more.")**

"How we get results is [INSERT METHODOLOGY]."

You may want to include:
- Number of appointments
- Facility benefits
- Client success stories

_____

_____

_____

_____

_____

_____

Step 6. Reveal how your "why" story speaks to them. **(Audience is thinking: "How do you know this on a deeper level?")**

"I know this to be true on a deep level because [INSERT 'WHY' STORY]."

_____

_____

_____

_____

_____

_____

Step 7. Give them a call to action. **(Audience is thinking: "Okay, how do I begin?")**

"The next step is [INSERT ONE OF THE ACTIONS THAT PEOPLE CAN DO RIGHT AWAY]."

Chapter 9
Step 1.
Why Should I Listen?
Lead with Their Need

"The difference between the right word and the almost right word is the difference between lightning and the lightning bug."

– Mark Twain

Picture it: your audience is sitting in front of you. They are potential clients or customers. Here's the way I see it. If there are five or fewer adults in your audience, they will remain adults, exhibiting the sophisticated behavior of giving you their attention. In my thirty years of speaking in front of groups, I've found that a group numbering more than five can transform into the kindergarten children I used to teach in the lab school at Columbia University. They twitch in their seats, check their electronic devices, talk to each other, and are generally distracted by shiny objects and everything else. So you need to begin your presentation with enough energy to grab them so that they will listen to you.

Besides the distracted ones, some have their arms folded across their chests, heads cocked to the side, looking at you sideways.

The question lurking in their minds is, "Why should I listen? What's in this for me?"

Your purpose in the opening of your speech is to literally get your audience to uncross their arms and lean forward. The first words out of your mouth need to prove to your audience that you know them. You are familiar with their needs, with the pain that you can alleviate, and the solutions you can bring to their situation. The opening of your presentation, regardless of the length of your speech, needs to grab them where they live so that they will uncross their arms, lean forward, and even poke a buddy next to them and say, "Wow, she knows me. She knows my pain. She has done her homework."

Before you speak, you need to do the real work—embrace the grind as athletes say about practice. You need to do the work of finding out about your audience. Research! Google is your best friend. Talk to people: previous speakers, the person who invited you, audience members who will be there. Don't be afraid to ask questions; the more you know your customer, the more your words will flow.

Here's an example. My opening for the speech related to this book often begins, "Does the thought of speaking in front of a group like this for more than thirty seconds make you sweat and keep you up at night? Do you suspect you may be boring? Do you wish you could make people laugh?" The beauty of the questions in this opening is that they actually invite responses from my audiences. It also invites a variety of responses for different situations. Some clients have told me that when they heard my opening, they decided to enroll from the get-go. These are the people who are terrified by public speaking.

Other clients tell me they are okay in front of a room but do suspect they are boring. So my second sentence is the one that makes them walk up to me and say, "I think I need you." Still others say they aren't "hooked" until they hear my last sentence about making people laugh. Lots of people don't know how to be humorous, and this is something they haven't wanted to admit.

Another one of my opening lines is, "Picture it: the elevator doors close. Uncomfortable silence fills the elevator. The person next to you turns to you and asks *the* question, 'So what do you do?' Is the first word out of your mouth, 'Um ...'?" This opening strikes another chord and touches on the fact that most of us don't have a prepared answer to that all-too-common question.

My client who owns a wellness facility uses this opening: "Do you *love* looking at yourself in the mirror ... *naked*? I didn't think so. Do you find your stomach tells you that you *can't* eat what you used to enjoy eating? Are you *sick* of doctors telling you these are normal signs of aging?" This is a gutsy opening, but this woman knows her audience. They are women over fifty, and they not only relate, they enjoy a good chuckle at themselves.

Here's another approach from a client whose purpose is to recruit consultants for network marketing of skin-care and nutritional products. "You know how, when you used to work for corporate America, you would get up every morning and think, 'Oh no'? And then you left corporate America, and you were your own boss and you thought that was the solution. And now, sometimes you wake up being your own boss with all the responsibility and you go, 'Oh no!'"

These clients instantly grab their audience with their opening words by touching upon the audience's need or pain. You're going for a few groans and chuckles from the audience. That's when you know you have them.

Chapter 10
Step 2.
So What's Your Solution?
Offer Your Solution

*"Who you are speaks so loudly
I can't hear what you're saying."*

– Ralph Waldo Emerson

Picture it: your audience has now uncrossed their arms, and they are leaning forward. The question in their mind is, "Okay, you got me. You seem to know my need. How are you going to help me?"

Now you get to provide a solution to the problem uncovered in Step 1. Here's where you use some words from your website home page or brochure. The best way to begin this part of your speech is to say, "I can help." Just like all fans of the BBC show *Doctor Who* know that Doctor Who cannot resist those two words, "Help me!" so it is that real people can't resist when they hear, "I can help." My Step 2 goes like this: "I can help. I'm Mimi Donaldson, your speech coach." (Use this if you have not been introduced by another person). "We will craft your perfect marketing speech. You will channel your nervousness into positive energy and use a formula for writing your presentation in less time and with less stress."

Here's Step 2 from the client who owns the wellness facility: "I can help. In my private healing sanctuary and fitness facility featuring top-of-the-line equipment, I transform lives through movement and motion because your mind is your body, and your body is your mind."

Here's Step 2 from the network-marketing client: "I can help. I will let you know about another place you can be. There's a place in the middle—between corporate America and being your own boss. I call it 'your happy place.'" These clients (and others) get their audiences to relax a little, lean forward, and ask the next question in their minds.

Use Speaking Language

You must change long sentences to shorter ones. I cannot stress this enough: *writing language is not speaking language.* People who are listening cannot look back several sentences to find out what you are talking about. No matter how much you like three-syllable words, if they are not in common use, you can't use them.

You can't say phrases such as "field of inquiry." People aren't used to hearing that phrase. That's a writing phrase.

Here are other phrases you can't say:
- "The dominant models for learning"
- "It becomes a political gambit." *Gambit* is a great word, but not for speaking.
- "Funneling the data"
- "There's something in his seemingly incessant demands that communicates he doesn't want to work on the project."

Chapter 11
Step 3.
Why Are You the One?
Here's Why

"If you don't toot your own horn, don't complain that there's no music."

– Guy Kawasaki

Picture it: your audience realizes that you know their problem and are offering a solution. The next question that pops into their minds is, "Okay, I see. But why are *you* the one that I should work with or buy from? Aren't there a whole lot of *you* out there? Aren't there many speech coaches, fitness-facility owners, network-marketing managers, attorneys, doctors, realtors, and veterinarians out there?" In this step, you have to call forth the credentials that make you stand out among your peers. Before people spend money on you, they want to know what gives you the right to ask them for it.

This is not a time to tell them the boring stuff, e.g., schools where you received your degrees and a list of companies you worked for in the past. If you're speaking for more than five minutes, I suggest you write an introduction with all of that information in it so that someone else can read it before you speak. To write your speaker introduction, see the "Now What? Take Action; Get Speeches" chapter for the "Introduction Template."

Highlight Why You're Unique

This is a time to highlight your unique credits that distinguish you from others. Here's an example of my Step 3: "Together, we will use my thirty years of keynote speaking with celebrities in front of audiences of thousands to craft your perfect marketing pitch." Very few people have that depth and breadth of experience, and that's what makes me unique and credible.

Here's Step 3 from the client who owns the wellness facility: "I've been doing this work for thirty-six years—since I was twenty years old. I'm fifty-six years old! I found that exercise and good nutrition made me more confident and vibrant, more energetic—without coffee! And you know when something feels so great you just have to share it? I wanted to share this with other people and do for them what I experienced. SO I got certified as a corrective exercise specialist and holistic lifestyle coach."

Here's Step 3 from the network-marketing client: "I was drawn to this business after twenty years in corporate America. I was in both sales and marketing. When I developed a video game to help kids combat childhood obesity, I met the First Lady, Michelle Obama, several times. When she thanked me, I realized I wanted more of *that*! I realized my sales and marketing expertise had to have a larger purpose. I wanted to impact people more directly than in a corporate job. In network marketing, I have the opportunity to empower people to start and maintain their own successful businesses."

These clients (and others) give the audience a sense that they are well qualified and worth listening to. The audience is ready for the next step, which is "give me a taste of your product or service."

Chapter 12

Step 4.

Okay, Prove It. Give Me a Taste. Here's Some Proof.

"Leadership is more a matter of consistency than charisma."

— Peter Drucker

Now your audience is listening because you've touched on a need and a solution. You've given them the evidence that you're the one they want. Now it's time for the part that you might think of as "your speech." This is the part that outlines the features and benefits of your product or service, statistics, and testimonials from past successes. The first three steps served to set up the potential client to receive the information that follows. Steps one through three were where you handed the glass of water to the audience. Now, steps four and five are where they reach out to take the glass of water—the information or content.

There are many ways to support your product or service. A good analysis of your audience will help you determine the proper mix of support points right down to choosing the words themselves! Tell them only what *they* need to know, not everything you know.

Be the Expert

You need to be the expert on your product or service by knowing 100 times more information about your product or service than you will ever say in a presentation. My client supplies her low-fat muffins to two large international chains. She needs to know the history of the muffin—no kidding. There are some features of your business that do not "speak well." They look great on paper, but they are not exciting verbally. When I hear these verbal "no-no's," I comfort my clients by saying, "That's great stuff. It's for your book or your article."

Knowing 100 times more about your business than you will actually say will make the question-and-answer period a breeze. As you may know, it was knowledge that literally saved the life of Scheherazade, the legendary Arabic queen and storyteller. Sir Richard Burton, translator of *One Thousand and One Nights*, writes:

> Scheherazade had collected a thousand books of histories relating to antique races and departed rulers. She had perused the works of the poets and knew them by heart; she had studied philosophy and the sciences, arts, and accomplishments ... so the King kept Scheherazade alive day by day, as he eagerly anticipated the finishing of the previous night's story. During these 1,001 nights, the king had fallen in love with Scheherazade, spared her life, and made her his queen.

If public speaking does indeed scare people more than death, you can feel like you've saved your own life by being prepared.

Support Points

Support points should anticipate your audience's questions and objections. They can be:

Examples: Refer to a specific situation that illustrates and supports your idea.

"XYZ Corporation found itself in a similar situation and instituted my program. It became one of the most profitable companies in the industry in less than eighteen months."

Statistics: Use numbers to show comparisons and trends, costs, various kinds of savings, etc.

"Any product you put on your skin is absorbed into your body in twenty-six seconds—much faster than if you simply swallowed it."

Testimony/Authority: Cite any individual, organization, or publication that has credibility with your group.

I use the following testimonial from a high-powered financial advisor:

> She thanked me and told me that meeting me was transformational. She said, "Somehow we never think our story is strong enough or will have the impact to influence the lives of others. After our meeting, I realized you and I are part of that evolution to help women become economically empowered."

Analogies: Analogies can be dramatic and forceful when used properly. Analogies help people "see" your point through the technique of comparing it to something outside the issue. Analogies can be brief or elaborate. When longer or more extensive, be sure they are clear and well rehearsed.

Here's an example:

"The initial study done in 2010 reflected only the tip of the iceberg. Today, our recommendation gets below the waterline to deal with the larger issues."

Here's another:

"We considered using only Strategy A, but just as you wouldn't want to rely only on your forehand in tennis to win a game—no matter how good that forehand is—we added Strategy B to ensure the success of this program."

Facts: A fact is a verifiable reflection of reality *or* a form of reality that everyone in the audience believes.

"Nothing succeeds like success."

"You have to spend money to make money."

The support section (Step 4) is where you highlight the evidence your audience needs to hire you. Again, you will depend heavily on the audience analysis that you did so carefully during your preparation. If your potential clients are numbers people, you will use a lot of statistics. If they are "tell me a story" people, you will tell them client success stories. If they are impressed by big names and research, you will quote influential people who have espoused the same product or service you are selling.

This step is also where you can share your methodology of the benefits of your product or how you implement your service. For instance, this is the part of the speech where I explain, "In a few two-hour sessions, we will craft your thirty-second intro, your sixty-second intro, and your ten-minute marketing speech."

You can also go into more detail about your product or describe the gym or shop or facility in which you conduct your business. Here's an example from the wellness-facility owner: "In our innovative and progressive fitness and wellness facility, you create new beginnings and experiences. We assist you in an individualized health program to heal your body from the inside out."

Your audience may give signs that they are ready to buy. If the majority of the audience looks restless or seems to be looking for more, skip the next step. You may want to go directly to Step 6—your "why" story.

Chapter 13

Step 5.
Give Me More
Here's More Proof

*"Extraordinary claims require
extraordinary evidence."*

– Carl Sagan

If you are speaking for ten minutes or less, you will not need this step. But if you are speaking for more than ten minutes, here's where you can actually use PowerPoint, handouts, and even interactive exercises among the participants. See the chapter or suggestions on how to create lively PowerPoint presentations and handout materials.

Use an Interactive Exercise

You may want to use an activity to offer something besides your talking head and visual aids. This interactive exercise, called "paired sharing," gets people participating. It starts with a question related to your product or service.

My client speaks about reinventing yourself. He asks the audience, "How many of you have reinvented yourself at least once in your life?" He gets almost everyone in the audience to raise their hands. He goes on, "How many of you have days now that look different from days six months ago?" He gets at least half the room to raise their hands. Then he says, "Turn to the person next to you, and tell them how your typical workday has changed from six months ago. You will have one minute to do this. I will let you know when the minute is up, and you need to switch. The person with the shortest hair (or coolest shoes) goes first." You watch the clock, and after a minute, you say, "If you haven't yet switched, switch now." Then at the end of another minute, you say, "Alright, start wrapping it up please. ... Thank you. Please finish the thought or sentence you're on. ... Thank you. Please get ready to stop, please. ... Thank you. Ready ... stop." I have used these exact words for paired sharing in a group of 1,500, and they stopped when I said, "Stop." I always give instructions like this, in simple steps that are doable. Then you are in control of the room.

By now, you have the audience rockin' and rollin'. They are ready to buy!

Chapter 14
Step 6.
Why Do You Do What You Do?
Here's My "Why" Story

"There are only two ways to influence human behavior: you can manipulate it or you can inspire it."

— Simon Sinek

Picture it: your audience is full of the facts and figures you've just presented, so enough of the objective reasons to use your product or service. Now is the time when people want to know the story *behind* the story.

When you speak for more than five minutes, an important story to include tells *why* you are doing what you are doing, or selling what you are selling. What is it that lights your fire? Where does your juice come from? What's at the *heart* of your business? People want to know.

People Magazine

The public's thirst to "know" was recognized in the media when *People* magazine came out in 1974. The articles featured the celebrity *behind* what you see on TV or in the movies. *People* showed where celebrities live as well as their families—the things at the heart of the person, and the motivation behind why they do what they do and have all that they have. Since that time, fans not only *want* to know, they think they *deserve* to know the story behind the star.

And that gets us to your story. Some coaches will tell you to *lead* with *your story* in a presentation, and that will sell you and your product/service better than any other beginning. I don't agree. Unless you are very famous and your story *is* the speech, I say, "*Lead with the need*" of your potential client or customer. First, you talk about *them*. When they like you well enough to want to know about you, then you talk about *you*. Then your story is appropriate. I say place it right before the call to action. It humanizes you even more.

Start with Why

Simon Sinek wrote a great book on this subject: *Start with Why*. I first saw him speak on this subject in his TED Talk. Sinek says those who tell their *why* story never manipulate; they inspire. And people follow them not because they have to; they follow because they want to.

So think about why you do what you do. We all have a "why" story. My dad had a very straightforward "why" story. His dad, a physician, died at age forty-six of massive heart disease. So my dad became a heart doctor—internal medicine.

Some of my clients have obvious stories from childhood that led to their career path today. One of my clients has that kind of "why" story. She grew up very poor. When she was in elementary school, she got permission to take home the unclaimed clothes from the lost and found before they were discarded. She would restyle the clothes with new lines and buttons, and she would add other pieces—making the clothes "cool" and oh-so attractive and desirable. This was her greatest pleasure. It's no mystery that her present business follows this path. She has been redesigning clothes all her life, and now she is a fashion designer. She does what she's always done and makes money doing it.

Another of my clients was a schoolteacher. One of her students had witnessed a traumatic event in his family and needed help. My client didn't have the skills to help this family in need, but she went back to school and is now a therapist. Her "why" was the realization she wanted to do more than reading, writing, and arithmetic.

Your "Why" Makes You Unique

Often your "why" story can distinguish you from others who are selling the same product or service. I have three clients who each sell the same leading brand of botanically based personal care products. Their ten-minute speeches are completely different, focusing on a different aspect of the business. The unique aspect they chose is exactly related to their "why" story.

The first woman says this: "So you may be asking, why am I so passionate about being healthy inside and out? Well, this is not a new consciousness for me. When my kids were four and six, I realized that proper eating would help them be better in school. I knew that McDonald's has a lot of junk in their meat.. My kids are now twenty-three and twenty-five and very healthy. They are very much aware of how important healthy choices are to a healthy lifestyle.

"Fast forward to the present. Two years ago, I started a journey looking for better skin care for my mom, who has Parkinson's. I wanted to find products that would be better for her nervous system and would not interfere with her current medications. Choosing a brand that was botanically based is very important to me and my family. Also important is choosing a greener, cleaner, safer product, which leaves a smaller carbon footprint for the future."

The second woman, mentioned in previous chapters, highlights the value of network marketing and loves to empower women to be independent. Her heart story is this: "What I love most about network marketing is that I really get to empower women to be independent. There I was on Skype with this woman in Poland, and she told me her story. She was the Director of mMarketing at Porsche-Poland. When her parents got sick and had limited time left to live, she quit her job at Porsche-Poland. But she needed to do something else to make money. She told me that she had two daughters that were four and six years old. Well, guess what? I told her that I had two sons that were also four and six years old. We laughed.

"So there we were, in the middle of working out her deal, and I realized why this story meant so much to me. She was Polish and I am Ukrainian. My parents brought me to this country when I was two years old. Her name was Aleksandra. My father's name is Alex, which is the male version of Aleksandra. When she started apologizing to me—'My English is not perfect'—the connection was complete. When my parents came over from the Ukraine, their English was not perfect. They went through a heartbreaking process of finding jobs because of it. In the Ukraine my mom was an architect. My dad was an engineer. They had prestigious jobs. But here, they were immigrants whose English was not perfect. They had to take blue-collar jobs to raise me and my sister. My mother, trained as an architect, does nails and toes. She is a manicurist. Mom would always say, 'Solnichka (this means *sunshine* in Russian), you must study hard and get a graduate degree, so you will not have a life as hard as your father and me.' I did just that. Thanks Mom."

The third woman who sells the same product shares her "why" story: "In 1982, I had breast cancer for the first time—the first time of four times in as many years. In the '90s, the doctors told me, 'You will die within five years.' I must have been depressed, but I remember saying to myself, 'I'm gonna party!' And I did. But I looked for healthy products. A friend told me, 'If you change your style of living and what you eat, you will stay healthy.' So finding natural products for health and wellness was my number one priority. My search for health led me to these wonderful, pure, safe, and beneficial products that are botanically based, using cutting-edge technology."

At this moment you may not have a clear-cut "why" story like the ones above. I didn't have a clear "why" when I started working—I discovered my "why" along the way. I was a drama major in college, and I thought I wanted the bright lights of Broadway. Only after teaching kindergartners for a couple years did I realize the bright lights I wanted were in their eyes. When children learn to read, it's called "unlocking the code." The light comes on in their eyes the moment they realize that the letter "b," signified by the stick with a circle at the bottom, sounds a certain way and stands for the first sound in "bat" or "baby."

Later, as a human resources trainer, I saw the eyes of managers light up when they learned that praising an "employee" in a role play made that "employee/actor" sit up a bit straighter and want to cooperate. I saw my name up in lights, but it's about lighting up the eyes. My speech coaching today is direct, one-on-one, and I see clients' eyes light up all the time with insight, excitement, and discovery. The first time a client told me, "In my speech, I said the sentence we wrote, and it got a laugh from the group," and his eyes lit up, I was hooked.

Please get in touch with me! Together, we will discover your "why" if you don't already know it. Then, we can position your "why story" in your marketing speech for best results. Check out my contact information at the back of this book in or email me directly at Mimi@MimiDonaldson.com

Chapter 15
Step 7.
Call to Action
How Do I Get Started?

"Honesty is the best policy."

– Proverb

Telling your "why" story is the perfect step before the call to action. It inspires rather than manipulates your audience. They now know your human story, and you may have given them a laugh or a tear. They are now inspired to give back something to you.

Always Be Closing

The end of the speech is the time to ask for a specific action. However, your attitude throughout the speech should be, "At any time during my presentation, someone in the audience is deciding to use me and my services." You want to be looking for encouragement from audience members who are smiling at you and nodding their heads. Always be closing.

Your Call to Action

Let's start with the dictionary (Wikipedia) definition of "call to action":

> In marketing, a **call to action** (CTA) is an instruction to the audience to provoke an immediate response, usually using an <u>imperative verb</u> such as "call now," "find out more," or "sign up today."
>
> A CTA can be a simple, non-demanding request like "choose a color" or "watch this video," or a more demanding request. An obvious CTA would be requesting the audience to purchase a product or provide personal details and contact information.

So your call to action is an explicit appeal to your audience to take a specific action following your speech. You may ask them to:

- Buy your product
- Sign up for your service
- Visit your website
- Fill out your survey
- Join your group
- Attend your webinar
- Call for a complimentary consultation
- Call for a twenty-minute free assessment

Be prepared with your CTA! Make sure it is clear, specific, and time-related. Do *not* ramble.

Here are some examples:

"To get us started, what we need is your approval today."

OR

"The next step is for us to have a conversation about how to improve your _____ (health/bottom line/marketing plan) ...."

Then be quiet! Resist the temptation to talk further. Don't explain or elaborate. Don't ask for questions. Let them digest what you have said. Give them time to grant you what you want. If they have any questions, they will ask. They always do.

If you are running a seminar or teaching a class, you may want questions.

See the section on Q&A.

So now you have a viable speech, but you're not done yet. This is where the hard work begins. It's called practice. The more you read your speech over and over, the better it will flow. You will have more fun, and so will the audience. I find this my biggest challenge working with clients: getting them to practice. The old saying keeps popping into my mind: "You can lead a horse to water, but you can't make him drink." There are no shortcuts here; you need to do the hard work of practice.

You can't force the horse to drink, but you can salt the oats. That's my job—to salt the oats. I want to inspire, not manipulate you to practice, practice, practice until your speech, from beginning to end, comes out looking and sounding effortless. You can do it. It's called mastery, and it will open doors you never imagined.

Part 3
Connect with Your Audience on Many Levels

"Don't ask questions that you don't want the answer to."

–John Henry Reese

Chapter 16

What if You Have Less than a Minute?

"A friend may be waiting behind
a stranger's face."

– Maya Angelou

Your 30-Second Speech and Your 60-Second Speech

As a speech coach, I hear this a lot: "Help! I know I need a thirty-second introduction at networking meetings. What do I say? How do I start? What do I leave out?"

I have a simple, three-step formula for you. The main goal is to follow the listener's frame of reference. What are they thinking when you first get up there? Well, contrary to popular belief, they're not thinking, "Who are you?" They don't care about you—YET. Most people start with, "Hi, I'm Mimi Donaldson, and I'm a speech coach, and I have a Master's degree, and over thirty years of experience, and yadda, yadda, yadda." They don't care yet. They care about, "Why should I listen? What's in it for me?" That's your audience.

Picture their arms folded tightly across their chest. Your job is to say something that will get them to unfold their arms. So what do you say? You have to identify a need, problem, or situation that will resonate with them. So if somebody asks me in the elevator, "What do you do?" I say, "You know how some of your friends love their business, but hate speaking about it in front of people?" They always go, "Yeah!" or they say, "That's me—I hate speaking." But what they're really saying is, "Okay, you got me." Now they know that you *know* something about them.

The next thing that pops into the person's mind is, "Well, how are you going to help me? What do you have?" So you offer your short solution. I say, "I help people create the perfect marketing speech so that other people love your business as much as you do." They can follow that. You've "got" their problem; you've given them a short but relevant solution.

Finally now, Step 3, they're thinking, "Well, uh, who are you? Why are you the one to help me? Aren't there a lot of *you* out there?" *That's* when you bring up your credibility. *That's* when you give your background and expertise. *That's* when you say, "Together, we will use my thirty years keynote speaking to audiences of thousands to craft your perfect marketing speech." That's credibility. Those three things will equal thirty seconds, and there it is. You lead with their need, offer the solution (according to your business), and answer the question, "Who are you?"

Real-Life Examples

Here's the thirty-second intro speech from the wellness-facility owner: "Do you *love* looking at yourself in the mirror ... *naked*? I didn't think so. Do you find your stomach tells you that you *can't* eat what you used to enjoy eating? Are you *sick* of doctors telling you these are normal signs of aging? I can help. I'm Patricia Garza, and I own Transformotion, an innovative and progressive fitness and wellness facility. We assist you in an individualized health program to heal your body from the inside out."

Here's the thirty-second intro speech from the skin-care professional: "Ya know how we are focused on food that's safe? But what about the things we slather on our skin day in and day out? Your skin is your largest organ. Anything you put on it is absorbed into your body in twenty-six seconds—faster than if you swallow it. I'm Bridget Stennis with Arbonne International. Please see me to find out about the healthiest, purest, and safest choice in skin care."

If you have sixty seconds, you can go to Step 4 and answer the next question in their mind, which is, "How do you get results—the solution to my problem?" Then you can give them a little information about your business and your methodology. Example: "The program for crafting your thirty-second speech and twenty-minute chamber speech is a few short private sessions in my home office."

The Real Elevator Speech

Let's be real. You don't have thirty seconds in an elevator with a stranger—you have fifteen. So when they ask you, "What do you do?" you have a few seconds to answer. And your energy level has to match theirs, so you can't be as "big" as you are at your networking meeting with twenty people in the audience.

In a very low-key tone you say, "Ya know how ...,"and then you fill in the problem people have that you solve. For me, it's "Ya know how some people hate speaking in front of a roomful of people?" And I stop and they say, "Yeah ... me" or "Not me, but my sister-in-law." Then I say, "I help with that."

Then they ask, "How?" and I say, "I'm a speech coach." And that's all the time I have. Now, hopefully, they will get off at my floor to find out more.

Here are a couple other examples. Financial consultant: "Ya know how some of us are worried we will outlive our money? Well, I help with that." Founder of charity for at-risk girls: "Ya know how we're worried about young people and their futures? Well, I help with that."

Your Kids Need an Elevator Speech

My advice: spread the word! Everyone who cares about you needs an elevator speech for you, just in case someone says, "Your friend, Mimi, what does she do?" Relationships make business happen. Start asking your friends for their one-liners about what they do. Then give them yours. Even your children need a one-liner in words they can understand. An example is my brother-in-law sold insurance when his first son was born. Little children cannot possibly understand the concept of insurance, but Randy made it understandable for Adam. And it paid off. Randy was standing on the sidelines of Adam's soccer game when Adam was five years old. One of the other fathers sidled up to Randy and said, "Hey, my son said your son told him, 'My daddy makes sure your daddy has money when he's old.' What do you do?" It was a perfect opportunity for Randy to tell this guy about his business. And yes, he did get the man as a client—and a couple other fathers too.

Here are more examples:

- "My aunt helps people talk about their business in front of lots of other people."
- "My mom takes care of your pet when it gets sick."
- "My dad helps you get healthy and feel good."

What's your one-liner? Write it down. Perfect it. Memorize it. Share it.

Chapter 17
Finding the Funny

"Humor is emotional chaos
remembered in tranquility."

– James Thurber

Why Find the Funny?

As professionals, most of us are accustomed to presenting material to varied audiences. We have an idea how to create relevant, timely, and effective content to get our ideas accepted and approved. We are pretty good at presenting ourselves with self-confidence and professionalism to attract our ideal clients. But hang on, there's more.

Have you heard the word "infotainment?" Here's the deal: The truth is if you're not funny, people won't want to listen to you. This is a whole new world. People want entertainment value. There's a running joke among professional speakers. Question: "Do I have to be funny?" Answer: "Only if you want to get paid!" Chances are, you're not a paid speaker, and adding humor is a major challenge for most people. Because many business professionals perceive humor to be so difficult, the most common tactic is to either tell a joke or *avoid* even making an attempt to be funny. This is

93

unfortunate. Using humor energizes your audience and increases the buy-in factor.

People retain information better when it entertains them. Your audience thinks, "If you can get an important idea across to me and make me laugh at the same time, I'm going to remember it—and you." Do we crave entertainment while being "taught"? Yes! There was a time when Southwest was the only airline that used laughter and fun to keep passengers listening. Now even straight-arrow Delta Airlines uses humor in their on-screen passenger briefing—lots of it.

Conventional wisdom is that some people are just "naturally" funny; they have the gift of saying things in a funny way. I don't think so. The funny person doesn't have a gift others lack. What they do have is the ability to *see the funny* in everyday life, and write it down, and use it. Your job as an effective speaker is to train yourself to see the situation and notice what's funny about it. When you can "mine" everyday humor—funny things that happen—your material will be unique. Unlike a joke, which audience members may have heard, your eye for humor makes your message unique.

In my book *Bless Your Stress*, I ask the readers to look at a happening-now stressful situation and ask themselves, "What's the blessing here?" My example: while sitting in a traffic jam, the blessing is that I'm not in a hospital room! Granted, I did not realize this until I actually *was* in a hospital room *wishing* I was in a traffic jam—in my car, wearing my clothes, eating what I wanted, hearing the sounds I wanted to hear ... you get the point.

Why Use Humor? It's Good for Your Life and Your Speech

1. Laughter is good for the health of your audience. It relaxes the whole body, boosts the immune system, and triggers the release of endorphins, which promote a sense of well-being. Who doesn't want that in a potential client?

2. Sharing the pleasure of original humor creates a sense of intimacy and connection between two people—qualities

that define solid, successful relationships. Notice how often people end up together in an intimate relationship because "he/she made me laugh." Just as humor keeps things exciting, fresh, and vibrant in a relationship, it can have the same effect on an entire audience.

3. Laughter is contagious. Just hearing one or two people chuckle can make the whole audience laugh. It can win over the tough customers who are not sure they like you— make them laugh and they'll think you rock.

When you make your listeners laugh, you have given them a gift. They feel a connection with you and are more likely to "feel" like giving you a gift back—their business.

How Can You Be Funny?

First, you must assume "something funny is going on." This is my ground of being. And if I don't see it as funny right now, I know it will be funny later because I say: "Pain plus time equals humor." How do I know this? From life! You know this too. Our situations that were painful five years ago are often funny now. The client who drove you nuts years ago now makes for a very good story. Disclosing an awfully embarrassing moment can create a story bond between you and another person.

Start collecting these painful moments—no kidding. I have them in a file, a manila file folder, because I started collecting them in the '80s before computers became the place for files. It all started with a letter from an audience member following my speech at a national meeting. The letter was *not* fan mail—just the opposite. It was tinged with anti-Semitism, including the phrase "Jewish fishwife." Distraught, I called my mother. "Mom, I'm so upset. Should I call the association and complain?" "Miriam," she said, "first of all, consider the source. Don't lower yourself to her level. Just put it away in your Insanity File and never think about it again." Good advice, eh? Mom meant file it away deep behind my brain, but I took her literally. I labelled the tab on a manila folder "Insanity

File," stuck the letter in there, and filed it away between the "H" and the "J." The file has grown over the years, with letters and e-mails printed out from impossible clients, vendors who thought I owed them money, and people who just wanted to vent. The "Insanity File" is very thick now. There are actually two. Occasionally I will look at it, and most of the items are quite hilarious now.

There is funny stuff happening every day if you just stop to notice and write it down. If you don't want an "Insanity File" like mine, you can have a "Funny File" of things that were never painful, things that were simply funny from the start.

Humor has a structure. First is the setup: the background necessary for the listener to understand the punch line. The punch line is the humor trigger and should be the last word or phrase you say. You want to hide the surprise until the very end.

While I suggest not using jokes, here's an old one to illustrate the structure. "Why does the chicken cross the road?" Punch line: "To get to the other side."

3 Humor Techniques

Creating humor is a matter of sentence structure, timing, and editing.

Here are three humor techniques you can incorporate into your speech:

1. The act-out

This technique is widely used in comedy. You've even used it yourself, when you tell a story to a friend and you say, "So, then she said 'How could you?!'" You are acting out the shocked tone of voice. You are doing an act-out. Without the act-out, you would say, "So then she was so shocked, and she actually asked how I could do this to her ... in a tone." That's describing the scenario in narrative fashion. It's not funny. Where you get the funny is when you actually *perform* the actual dialogue, vocal tone, and personality of the person.

For example, in my speech about men and women, I tell a story about when the testosterone of a three-year old boy kicks in, and he discovers he no longer likes "shopping with mom." It goes like this: "No sooner have they gotten into the mall, but he stops dead, stomps his little cowboy boot on the mall floor, and says, 'Um ... um ... Mom [and I do the three-year-old's little sounds and tone], do you *know* where we're going, or are we just gonna ... wander around?'" I do my best three-year-old face throughout, with the habit they have of forming their words very carefully, using their little lips in an exaggerated fashion. The audience always cracks up. Act-outs are performed in present tense, which is so much funnier than past tense or narrative.

Pay attention to small children; they are a great source of humorous incidents. And watch any episode of John Oliver's show on HBO, *Last Week Tonight*. He uses one act-out after another.

2. Series of 3

Here is a useful structure for humor writing. In a two-person comedy act, the straight person sets up the pattern that the funny person will break with the punchline. The first sentence sets up the funny sentence. The series of three uses a similar structure. The first two items set the pattern, and the third one breaks the pattern with a twist, a curve, the unexpected. An example from George Carlin: "I live in Florida. Everything is in the eighties: the temperature, the ages, the IQs."

Here's an example I use in a speech when I talk about diversity of styles. "Some people have a formal time style. They are formal with time. You know who you are. You are always early—at least twenty minutes early. Your partner, most likely, is casual with time. They can't understand why you want to be so early. But we formal people—and I'm one of you—know why. We are the designated worriers of the relationship.

"We have impending-disaster scenarios in our heads like, 'What if ... there's traffic? What if ... the car breaks down? What if ... the freeway is ... GONE!?" Big laugh. Why? Series of three. Traffic is plausible. So is the car breaking down, but less so. These first two are the buildup to the third in the series—the punch line. "The freeway is gone" is hardly plausible, but because of the buildup, it's funny.

3. The call-back

Another technique comedians use is called the "call-back." You literally call back a previous phrase or sentence so that it becomes sort of a rally cry. It's a technique that creates a closer connection with your audience, helps them remember your material, and possibly gets you a laugh.

For example, in my speech about men and women, I tell a true story about men wanting to save face and not asking for directions. I urge women not to point out when men have lost face—not a good idea. In that story, I'm in the car with a male companion, and he says, "I know a shortcut ...," and then follows that with "hmm ... it doesn't look like 'west,'" and I say to the audience, "I don't say anything—I know better." After each of his further statements (indicating he has no idea where we are) that I act out, I say, in the same tone of voice, "I don't say anything—I know better." The second time I "call back" that sentence, the audience laughs, and by the third time—they roar.

The call-back in a speech doesn't have to refer back to something funny in order to be effective, it just has to connect with the audience emotionally. In my football book speech, I tell the story that got me hooked on the value of football, and all sports, for women. My boyfriend pointed out, "The whistle blew—the play is over." It gave me pause. I point out to the audience how important that is for women, and we need to have short memories. All of us need not drag the bad stuff into the next moment; we need to shake off the bad plays and move on. During the forty-five-minute speech, I repeat the sentence, "The whistle blew—the play is over," and each time, the response is a reverent quietness from the audience. I know they "got it."

Repetition builds relevance and reinforces the relationship between the speaker and the audience.

Chapter 18
Do You Need Visual Aids?

"A picture is worth a thousand words."
– Proverb

Visual aids are meant to do just that—to "aid' you in your talk. Visuals are not meant to replace you or your message. They emphasize, clarify, and reinforce what you have to say. You, the speaker, not the visuals, should drive the presentation. Be careful of "death by PowerPoint" by using slides with too much text or too many charts and graphs that are too tiny to read. It's a disservice to say, "If you could see this ...."

Over 80 percent of what we know comes to us visually. Words involve a listener's left-brain functions; what they see involves their right brain. When you speak and show a visual, you are engaging both sides of the listener's brain and making a greater impact than you might have otherwise. With any presentation lasting over an hour, people need something else to look at besides you.

Visuals can also help keep you on track and keep you from rambling or losing your place. Research shows that the purely visual part of your PowerPoint presentation will contribute 55 percent of the impact on your audience. What you say contributes 38 percent, and the text you quote on a page contributes 7 percent. So the case for using visuals is very strong!

Tips on Preparing PowerPoint

1. When preparing visuals, the most important point is: Know your audience. Do they need charts or graphs? Do they respond to cartoons? Use the audience analysis sheet. Prepare your visuals after you write your speech, not before. Remember, they are called visual "aids." The purpose of a visual aid is to support the speaker's message while stimulating the listener's mind and imagination. You, the speaker, not the visuals, should drive the presentation. Don't make the slides the focus. They are there to provide supplementary information.

2. The slides should be in a steady narrative stream—one per step. Each slide supports a point you are making. Use no more than ten slides for a twenty-minute speech, and no more than fifteen to twenty slides for an hour-long speech.

3. The best visual aids are pictures, not words because the brain adds content to the picture. People tend to remember pictures better than words.

4. Letters and pictures should be large enough to be easily seen from the back of the room by everyone. Use nothing smaller than a thirty-point font.

5. Make your visuals simple and uncluttered. Each slide needs to be easy to read with a lot of white space. If you use words, limit the text to five to seven lines per visual, and five to eight words per line. Avoid full sentences—and no paragraphs, please. Less is better.

6. Use color on your visual aids for variety and interest. Bright colors such as red, yellow, or green are best.

7. Be accurate. Spell-check everything! Don't give any nitpicker in the audience a reason to disapprove. The same goes for punctuation. Make sure your grammar is correct.

8. Some techniques control the flow of information. They can add variety and dramatic impact to your message. One of them is progressive disclosure, or "builds" in which bullet points are revealed one at a time as you reach them. With the first click of your PowerPoint, Item #1 is shown and discussed. Then Item #2 is shown along with #1. Then Item #3 is shown along with #2 and #1. Often the new item appears in a new color for contrast and emphasis.

Handout Materials

Handouts serve several useful purposes for your presentation. You are offering a great deal of information during your talk, and it is nearly impossible for the audience to absorb everything you have to say. Handouts help make your presentation more memorable by giving participants something they can refer to later.

Some common examples of effective handouts are:
- A general outline of your talk or the program format
- Copies of visuals you will be showing; this is especially appreciated if you are showing charts, graphs, or other comparative material. Copies of these save the audience the time and trouble of copying such information from slides and allows them the freedom to listen to what you are saying.
- Reprints of pertinent articles written by you or others
- Bibliographies and other sources for further information

Never hand out verbatim copies of your presentation. This can produce negative reactions: "Why did I bother attending? I could have read the talk instead."

Can You Use Notes?

You have many choices as to how to deliver your presentation. You can read a prepared script, use note cards, use pictures or cartoons on cards to cue you, read the visuals to the group from the PowerPoint, or use a combination of techniques.

Let's examine each option.

1. Reading: Not recommended. It is boring to listen to someone read a prepared script, and in many ways it's an insult to your audience. Eye contact is virtually impossible.

2. Notes: Highly recommended. Each card (3x5 or 5x7) contains only key words or key phrases (not a full script) to cue you. You sound spontaneous, yet the notes keep you on track and prevent you from wandering. Be sure to number the cards. Use color to separate your main points on the cards. Color helps you find your place more quickly as well.

3. Combination of techniques: Recommended. Some people will have critical parts of a talk that must be said just so, e.g., legal announcements, sensitive issue announcements, quotations, and comments to the press. That part can be read (although you should still try to look at your audience). Use what works best for you and your audience.

Tips:
- Don't memorize—you'll sound stilted. Also, if you forget your next line, you will be utterly lost.
- However, you can—and should—memorize your opening and call to action.
- Write your notes on your visuals so that you can coordinate them effectively.
- Tape yourself if you can. Listen to and evaluate your speech.

- Remember the old saying: "How do you get to Carnegie Hall?" Answer: "Practice, kid, practice!" Likewise, to turn in a professional performance, you must practice. Do it in short bits, rather than working on the whole speech in one session, but do it!

Chapter 19
Questions and Answers

"Judge a man by his questions rather than by his answers."

– Voltaire

The main purpose of taking questions from the floor after speaking is to give the audience a limited opportunity to participate. When responding, your objective is to present yourself and your point of view as accurately, smoothly, and credibly as possible.

Because you are in charge of your presentation, you set the rules regarding the question-and-answer period.

Important guidelines:

- Keep your comments brief so that you can answer as many questions as possible.
- Limit each member of the audience to only one question.
- Keep your answers brief by picking the one point that you wish to emphasize.
- Don't get into a discussion with an audience member. If you do, everyone else will feel left out.

Here are the four steps for answering a question with grace and control:

1. RECOGNIZE

- Concentrate on the question being asked so that you understand it completely. Look directly at your questioner. Avoid the temptation to think ahead to formulate your answer. If you don't understand the question, ask for clarification. If the questioner uses a word or phrase that you don't understand, find out what it means.

- **Important note:** Never judge the question. It's so easy to say, "Good question," to the questioner. But unless you are going to say that to every questioner, don't say it to one—and you won't say it to every questioner because then you sound insecure, trying to gain favor. Besides, every question is not a good question.

2. REPEAT/REPHRASE

- Once you're sure you understand the question, you may need a few seconds to develop your answer. When speaking to groups of fifteen or more, you may gain some thinking time by repeating the question to the entire group. This also helps members of the audience who may not have heard the question when it was asked.

- Sometimes it's appropriate to rephrase, rather than repeat the question. If the question is too lengthy, rephrase it in your own words. If a question involves a slang word or phrase, it's best not to repeat it. Or if a hostile person asks a "loaded" question, rephrasing it will help you diffuse the hostility and maintain control.

✳ **EXAMPLE**

✳ **QUESTION**: Can you tell me why your organization makes it a practice not to hire over the age of forty?

✳ **ANSWER**: I'm being asked to comment on our hiring practices.

- In a small group or one-to-one situation, it is not necessary to repeat the question. You can gain time to frame your answer by verbalizing the general area of the question. For example, if someone asks how much your service will cost, you might respond by saying, "I've been asked about the cost effectiveness of my product."

3. RESPOND

- Always tell the truth.

- If you don't know the answer, admit it. Tell the person you'll find the answer and get back to him or her.

- Be clear in as few words as possible.

- Use evidence in answering the question (e.g., example, analogy, fact, statistics, experience).

- Make eye contact with your questioner at first, and then give your answer to the group, looking at different people as you speak.

- When you finish your answer, make sure you're looking at someone other than your questioner. Otherwise, he or she might ask you another one.

4. RECOGNIZE THE NEXT QUESTION

What if you can't answer a question? You just don't know. There's no sin in admitting this.

Remember the purpose of your presentation: to present yourself and your point of view calmly, smoothly, and credibly. Your goal in the question-and-answer period is to maintain your position as the leader of the group. There is no shame in saying, "I don't know, but I will find out."

Chapter 20

Hecklers

What do you do with hecklers? Your natural instinct might be to shrink away from a heckler or strike back. Some audience members might challenge, embarrass, or debate you. Your job is to be as informative as possible, clarifying points or giving requested information, not to engage in verbal wrestling matches.

Many speakers are thrown off balance when a member of the audience challenges them, often feeling compelled to defend or explain their positions. As soon as you start defending yourself, you not only lose psychological ground, but you risk sacrificing your credibility.

To avoid defending yourself, you must understand the rules of the game. Confrontational or embarrassing questions are seldom accidental. The intent of the questioner may be to throw you off guard, to upset you.

Here's my take on hecklers: this may sound weird, but I want you to **pretend you placed the heckler there.** This is the only way you're going to handle it gracefully. When the heckler starts, you have to listen closely and let go of any defensive attitude you may have. Now, if your point of view is that this person is a plant, then everything the heckler says can further your purpose. If the comment is intelligent, you can thank them for enhancing your point, or you can say something like, "Ahh," "Hmm," or "That's a thought."

Sometimes a questioner will challenge you by making what amounts to a speech of his or her own. When a question becomes a long dissertation, the audience member is trying to take over your leadership role. By all means interrupt. Don't wait for the speaker to finish. Count to three and say, "Would you be so kind as to rephrase that as a question?"

If the questioner persists in monopolizing the floor, count to three, interrupt again, and say, "Thank you for your contribution. May I have the next question?"

Most members of the audience will be delighted by your response. They, too, resent moves made to unseat the speaker. The longer you allow a member of the audience to monopolize attention, the more impatient the audience will be for you to reassert your control.

Remember, this is your time on stage. You have the right to interrupt any person who tries to take attention away from you and your presentation.

Sometimes those strategies work; sometimes they don't. What else can you do? Try to defer. You can say, "Of course if you have questions, please see me at the end." Or "It appears you have a unique situation. Let's discuss this one-on-one after my presentation so that your issue can be addressed." This works out because hecklers are usually the first people out the door. If you say, "I welcome questions throughout the presentation," then you'd better be prepared. I strongly suggest you *not* say that. It leads to a pet peeve of mine: speakers who put questions off. They say, "Yes, I'm going to answer that question later," which causes that audience member to think, "I don't want later; that's why I asked you the question *now*." It plays like a power trip—the speaker is more powerful than the audience. Never true. You will win the battle to lose the war.

Your audience is the customer. You are the one who wants something from the audience. Here's a great alternative. Say: "Okay, I hear your question. I'm going to deal with that one more extensively later, but let me give you the short answer *now*." Then save the long answer for later. This way you keep everyone happy.

If you can handle a heckler really well, it will convince any skeptical audience members of your poise and credibility. You may never get the heckler to your side, but you can impress the heck out of everybody else in the room. That's why hecklers are helpful. They help show other people how capable you are.

Chapter 21
What Can Go Wrong

*"The most important thing in communication
is hearing what isn't said."*

– Peter Drucker

What can distract you from getting it done?

Know the Laws of the Universe

When you're writing a speech, as when doing anything else, there are laws of time management you must keep in mind.

The first is Murphy's Law:

1. Everything takes longer than you think it will.

2. Nothing is as simple as it seems.

3. If anything can go wrong, it will.

So give yourself "recovery time" between tasks, and always overestimate the amount of time something will take.

The next one is Parkinson's Law:

C. Northcote Parkinson, a well-known English author, wrote: "Work tends to expand to accommodate the time allotted to it." Now what does that mean? If you say to yourself in the morning, "I've got the whole day to get this report done," how long will it take you? Yes, the whole day. But what if you say to yourself, "Omigosh, I've only got an hour to get this report done." How long will it take you? Yes, an hour.

If nothing is scheduled for a period of time, it's best not to consider it as "free time." All these other things you thought would take only a little while spilled over because you didn't schedule the entire day. Tip: schedule your priorities. This includes writing your speech.

People say, "If you want something done, give it to a busy person." The reason? Busy people stick it into their schedule and adjust everything around what needs to be done. That's how I handle exercise. There was a point where it became very important to exercise regularly to maintain my health. Scheduling it three times a week meant that everything else had to adjust around it. And it did and still does.

Your schedule could even include writing a book. To write this one, I cut back on my sleep. I used to get eight or nine hours, and I've cut down to seven or sometimes six because I needed to write. Make sure you fill your schedule with high-priority items so that other less important stuff doesn't spill over into your time.

Your Time is Your Inventory

A deadline is like a ticking clock with a bomb attached. Every sweep of the second hand brings you closer to the moment of detonation.

Of course, most of us don't have a single looming deadline in our lives. Most of us have *several* of them, maybe even one in every time zone. Get the report in, make that call, pick up the kids, pick up your spouse at the airport, wash and dry the cat (or was it the dog?). At home and at work, a lot of clocks are ticking, all day, all the time.

Most days, the bomb doesn't go off. Somehow you manage to defuse it, defer it, or delay it for some other day.

But that feeling, that coiling up of tension inside you as the clocks tick toward the "boom," that sensation of imminent doom takes its toll. Time, and our lack of it, is one of the great gut-wrenching elements of stress. It wears on your health and your ability to function in your job and your relationships. And it can derail an awesome speech.

Don't let time stress grind down your body and your effectiveness. You can tame it, once and for all. If you're ready to take action, read on.

Take Back Your Time

Reclaiming your time is the first step. Your time is your inventory (this is my favorite mantra). Without it, none of your skills are of any use at all. But once you assume control of your time, all your skills can be directed toward the results you want.

Maintaining ownership of your time, with your busy schedule and all the priorities competing for your attention (including the priorities of others), takes skill and practice. You must be deliberate about protecting your schedule from the time wasters that constantly threaten to divert you from what's really important.

Priorities are, by definition, activities that further your goals. You need priorities to get where you're going. Take a moment to clarify what your important items are. Speaking to grow your business definitely furthers your goals. This requires that you prioritize your activities and stick to your plan when writing your speech. Get rid of your biggest time wasters.

Let's focus now on the three real "biggies" of time wasting:

1. **INABILITY TO SAY "NO"** to potential time wasters.

2. **CRISIS** that is "externally initiated," that is, initiated by other people and situations

3. **PROCRASTINATION** that is "internally initiated," that is, by you. Of course, we'll save procrastination for last ...

How to Say "No"

How do you say "no" compassionately to potential interrupters or potential robbers of your time—the "got a minute" people: those who come to your office and say, "Got a minute?" They look like they need you. And you're such a wonderful person that you hate to put them off and say "no." But you have to say "no" when your priority is bigger than their interruption. Use what I call the "4-A Action Method."
The first "A" is "Acknowledge," the second "Advise," the third "Accept" (with limits), the fourth "Alter."
Here's an example.
Your co-worker says, "Got a minute?"

1. Acknowledge. You say, "I see you're upset. It looks like you need to talk to me."

2. Advise. You say, "Here's the situation. I have to finish this report first. It's due in half an hour."

3. Accept (with limits). You say, "I want to help—I just need a little time." Not recommended because the better choice is:

4. Alter. You say, "I'll come to your office as soon as I'm done with this report."

Your co-worker says, "Thank you."
You have successfully said "no," avoided the potential time-wasting conversation, and you've been thanked for it!

How to Handle Crisis

The dictionary definition of "crisis" is "an unexpected interruption of major impact, above and beyond the normal day's events, requiring immediate response." The problem, though, is not how we define the word "crisis." The problem is that we label incidents as crises that are not crises at all, causing us to throw our carefully established priorities out the window and run off to handle the supposed "crises." The irony is this has the potential to create a new, *real* crisis. Here are some examples:

- The supervisor labels the report due every Friday a crisis. This is not a crisis. The tip-off? *Every* Friday it's expected, so it's not a crisis. Tense and high-pressure, maybe. But that's a planning and organizing problem, not an unexpected crisis.

- A general manager labels her son falling out of a tree as a "crisis" only to learn he skinned a knee and is now eating cookies. Moreover, he falls out of the same tree every other day. This is not a crisis either. Why? Serious injury requiring parental intervention is a crisis; children falling is routine in this case, and not above and beyond the normal day's events.

- A salesperson is late for a sales meeting because she stopped to handle someone else's emergency. This is not her crisis. It did not "require" her immediate response. She chose to help someone and shoved her own priority aside in the process.

All of these people were duly stressed out (as were the people they kept waiting), so they used the word "crisis" to describe the panic they felt. But before you take on something as a crisis and let it dictate your priorities, remember these simple guidelines:

1. If it's not your crisis, return it to its proper owner.

2. Determine where the event you label "crisis" fits on your life's priority scale. Do you respond, delegate, or ignore and let its owner take care of it?

3. *Plan* for crisis. You can't if they're really unexpected, but very few events are totally unexpected. You can plan to

avoid or anticipate those "moments" by handling them calmly, or handing them over to the proper party.

A crisis planned is an event managed. Put a sign on your desk: "I cannot let your lack of planning become my crisis." This will remind you that your time is *yours*. It does not belong to anyone else.

To effectively help you plan for crisis management, I've created this easy-to-complete form that you can download here: http://www. pitchperfect.biz/

Next Time a Crisis Occurs

1. STOP—Push the pause button.

2. LOOK—Relate the crisis to one of your goals. Ask: "Does the action required relate to a high priority for me?"

3. LISTEN—to your inner voice.

    Ask yourself, "Who owns this crisis?"

    Decide whether to:

    Respond (ADAPT)

    Postpone (AVOID) or

    Delegate (ALTER)

    Base your decision on the value and consequences of each action.

4. Make your action plan.

5. Avoid being all stressed out in the next similar "crisis" by planning for fast detection and planned action.

Chapter 22

Positive Procrastination

Okay, we've put off "procrastination" until last. How appropriate. The definition is "to put off intentionally and habitually."

Let's lay negativity and panic aside. I think procrastination is a *positive* word that's gotten bad press. Some psychologists have noted that procrastinating signals poor self-esteem. Granted, if you put something off, you can never fail at it, but you can never succeed either. So I say be positive about procrastination. Look at the word itself. Even the prefix "pro" is positive. Notice all the positive words with the prefix "pro": *professional, proactive, procreate, prolong, profess.* When I asked for more of these words at a recent seminar, someone yelled out "Prozac!"

The point is procrastination does not put you in the position of being a victim of circumstances, like "crisis" can. "To put off intentionally" means you *meant* to put it off, and "habitually" means you put it off *more than once.* Procrastination is not the word of a helpless victim, yet we use it that way. We beat ourselves up for procrastinating. However, when we look at it truthfully, we must admit that the things we procrastinate about are usually things we don't want to do.

Two actions are possible:

1. Adapt your attitude. Cross the item off your list and stop thinking you "should" do it, or

2. Alter, by delegating the task.

But what if it's important for you to do it? What if it's a priority? You know the drill: break the task down into smaller, doable tasks, and do each of them one at a time. Reward yourself after each task. For some of us, drawing a line through that dreaded item on our "To Do" list is satisfying enough; others must promise themselves a coffee break or a piece of chocolate.

Be a proud procrastinator of the unimportant, unloved tasks. Put them off, and stop beating yourself up. And stop reacting in a panic mode to events you mistakenly label "crises." Remember: your time is yours. When you become a master of your time, you become a master of your life.

What if You Want to Quit?

Ever notice you barrel through, or stumble through, the meat of an assignment, but then, when it comes to putting on the finishing touches—BAM! Life gets in the way. The same principle applies to writing your speech. You wrote it, but now you must practice! That's where, I'm sad to say, too many people drop the ball. To achieve most things in life, even small ones (but especially big ones), you must have commitment and discipline. Commitment is the will to hold onto your objective with alacrity and to dedicate your time and energy to it. Discipline is the act of carrying out what you want to happen over time. It means finishing what you started—and not quitting.

Failures are just the steps to success. Don't believe it? Here are some examples:

Albert Einstein: He didn't speak until he was almost four years old, and his teachers said he would "never amount to much."

Walt Disney: He was fired from a newspaper for "lacking imagination" and "having no original ideas."

The Beatles: They were rejected by Decca Recording Studios, who said, "We don't like their sound—they have no future in show business."

Did these superstars lose heart? Did they take their foot off the gas? Or did they know they could beat the odds? YES!—they kept on keepin' on. This is the inspiration for all of *us*.

A Bout of the Doubts

And, just in case you have a "moment," or have a bout of the doubts about your speech, don't change anything within forty-eight hours of delivering your speech. Changes can throw you off, and your insecurity can communicate to your audience. Remember: don't make your audience nervous.

How do you stay positive when you have written your speech, and your noisy, inner critic keeps saying, "I'm not ready"? That's the noise in your head, and you now must stay poised in the noise. "Stay poised in the noise" is what NFL coaches preach to their teams when they are going to a loud stadium for an away game. The fans in many stadiums are *so loud* for the home team that the visiting team can hardly hear the quarterback calling signals. They figure out sign language to communicate. *We* need to answer the *noise* in our heads: "My speech isn't original enough," "I didn't practice enough," "*I'm* not enough." When I have those moments, *I thank my mind for sharing*, and then I move ahead. Commitment and discipline are what you need to say poised in the noise. And you must not quit.

We. Don't. Quit.

My mother drove home this lesson to me in high school during the Illinois High School State Speech Tournament. It was my senior year, and my school, Richwoods Community High School of Peoria, was in the finals at the University of Illinois campus. I was in the middle of my comedy reading event in a very hot, packed classroom when I went blank. The silence scared me and I felt faint. I stumbled toward the door of the classroom, opened it, and felt a whoosh of cool air. My mother was right behind me.

Using my "serious" name, my mother said, "Miriam, get back in there and finish!"

"No, Mom," I whined. "I can't. I'm too embarrassed."

Mom said, "We. Don't. Quit. Get back in there right now and finish." I flashed her a look; she was being rough on me, but the roughness was necessary. And she recited the last line of the routine I had uttered. I went back in, fought through the waves of pity I felt from the audience, and made them laugh once more. The judges didn't know what to do with me. I had placed first in Regionals, but there is a category called "Poise," and they had to mark me down for that. They gave me fifth place, which counted for one point for my team. That year my school won its first State Championship by—wait for it—one point. Really. If I had quit, I would not have been awarded that one point, and we would not have won. That's how important it was for me not to quit.

In my book *Necessary Roughness: New Rules for the Contact Sport of Life*, I tell this story in the context of sports. Professional football players come with commitment, discipline, and the no-quitting attitude already installed in their systems. They would have never been able to make the NFL without these characteristics. No one makes it into professional sports without them.

And in the world of business, those who succeed usually have the same kind of commitment and discipline as their athletic counterparts. In fact, you will often find that these business leaders are also big sports fans, as well as competitive athletes in their own right. These principles are that universal; success in the boardroom often walks hand in hand with success on the field. And success in the boardroom also depends on how well you express yourself.

So when "life" gets in the way, *thank life for sharing* and don't be distracted. Instead, channel my mother. Use your serious name, and say to yourself, "We. Don't. Quit."

How Do I Get Rid of My "Ums"?

Power of the Pause

There you are. Your speech is ready. You practice it. You audiotape it. You start to listen to it and—wait a minute. ... What are those sounds? To your horror, you hear yourself punctuating every sentence with "um" and "uh." It's the word equivalent of the photo bomb. How can you avoid this? Here's where the power of the pause comes in.

Using pauses during a presentation is a vital way to engage the audience and deliver your message effectively. Pausing feels uncomfortable, and it's difficult to do when we are up in front of a room.

We all know that speaking to an audience is different from everyday conversation. In everyday conversation, a pause signifies to the other person that someone else can start talking. We keep going, using filler words to indicate we have more to say. That's not the case when you are in front of a room. No one is going to interrupt you. So you don't need the "ums" and "uhs" and "ya knows" to hold the space.

It's much preferred (and far more powerful) to use the pause to punctuate your sentences. It says you are in control. It can serve as an exclamation mark, to underline a critical point. We do it with a colon in book titles. Example: *Bless Your Stress: It Means You're Still Alive!* is much better than *Bless Your Stress Means You're Still Alive*. The pause gives the reader time to digest and remember the important first part. The same goes for speaking. The pause allows the audience to involve themselves in your speech. It invites them to be part of your conversation, turning a one-way speech into a two-way connection.

Here's how to cultivate the power of the pause:

1. Become aware. Listen to yourself on tape (painful as it may be) to discover your filler words. Or ask a trusted friend or colleague—they already know.

2. Plan your pauses. Separate your speech into thought groups, and draw lines to divide your notes. When you see a line, you will naturally pause. The seven steps of the Presentation Formula are valuable here. Each step makes you pause and deliver the new step with more energy.

3. Pause at the end of each PowerPoint slide if you are using them. Pause at the ends of sentences and at the ends of paragraphs. You can pause between words for emphasis. Best. Advice. Ever.

4. Be prepared. This is the most important step, and it requires the most work. Notes are acceptable, but you need to *know* your speech so well that you can eliminate the uncertainty that makes you anxious. When you are anxious and insecure, you will use a filler, such as "um," to fill the space.

5. Be prepared to fill the pause with energy! If your voice trails off at the end of a sentence, the pause that follows makes the audience shift in their seats. They're not sure if you forgot or thought of something more important. The only way to energize the silence is to energize your words before—and after—the pause. So be passionate about your message, and if you're not, fake it till you make it. When you fake energy in speaking, you energize yourself. When you energize yourself, you energize your audience.

What if I Forget What to Say?

As a speech coach, I am often asked, "What do I do if I'm in the middle of a speech, and I forget what to say?" Here are three solutions:

1. Never write your speech out word for word. Don't memorize it word for word. That's a surefire path to disaster because if you trip up on one word, you'll lose your way completely. Instead, learn it in "thought groups." Each "thought group" will start with the "step" you wrote in part two of this book. Your speech will have seven steps. You will have at least seven "thought groups." Practice it enough so that you know what comes first, second, and third. That's where people mess up. They don't want to practice. It takes time and effort. Practice is the only way to master your material.

2. Use visual aids. Note cards are great. I use 4x6 note cards. The cards must be stiff enough so that they won't crinkle or make noise in your hands. Don't play with them. All you need is a note card with a thought group on it, the title of the story, or whatever is coming next. The audience feels secure knowing you know what comes next.

   Then there's PowerPoint. When you use PowerPoint, the next slide will guide you to the next thought. You can write in the margins of the PowerPoint on the hard copy. See thechapteron visual aids.

3. If you have a speech coach like me, you're going to get the best tool of all—the words in the formula that predicts and follows the listener's frame of reference or train of thought. This will guide you because it's logical. People will listen because you've connected.

And finally, here's a little bonus. When I'm speaking, there are rare occasions when I forget what I'm saying. I actually turn to one of the nodding people in the front row and say, "What was I talking about?" I really do! And they tell me, or their friend next to them tells me exactly what I need to know. I say, "Thank you," and move on. The audience loves it because now they know I'm human, and they can relate to me even more.

Remember, the audience is rooting for you! They are so glad you're up there and they are not!

Chapter 23
Now What?
Take Action; Get Speeches

"No legacy is as rich as honesty."
– William Shakespeare

Speak for Free

So, now you have your ten- or twenty-minute speech about your business. You have your thirty-second and sixty-second introductions for networking meetings. You have a professional introduction for the person introducing you if your speech is more than five minutes long. Now it's time to actually find opportunities to speak.

My most important advice is this: take every opportunity to speak. You will start out by speaking for free, and there are many places to do that. In one of my networking meetings, a business owner said, "I was asked to speak in Riverside, but that's so far away from where I live and work that I turned it down." I couldn't help myself. I said to her, in front of the group, "I would take every opportunity to speak. You never know who, in Riverside, knows people in your area. When you speak, it gives people an opportunity to know you, like you, and trust you." The other six people in the meeting nodded their agreement, and two of them said, "Mimi's right." I love when I'm right. The point is you never know how the stone you toss into the pool of people will ripple back to you in the form of profit.

To get the opportunity to speak for free, you should have a plan and develop a strategy. I enjoy networking meetings so much that I have gone as a participant to the meetings I want to speak for. My theory is that when people get to know you and get familiar with your expertise, they will jump at the chance to have you speak for free at their meeting. You can usually attend two or three meetings of an association, networking group, or service group without joining as a member. I suggest going to the meeting to familiarize yourself with the group.

Remember, if you're going to lead with their need, you need to know their need and how they speak about it. Listening to people in casual conversation is the best way to do your research. Important note: after you do speak, always attend the next meeting or two of the group. People who did not immediately sign on to buy your product or service will have thought about it over the past month. More times than not, I will close clients the month *after* I speak or the month *after* that. It seems they want to "touch" me a couple times before they invest in my service. Recently, I attended the next meeting after I spoke, and the speaker canceled at the last minute. When I walked in, the leader said, "Mimi, could you do an encore of your wonderful speech from last month?" Of course I could, and I got to do another call to action. Score!

Strategic Partners

Strategic partners are people who do not do what you do but are involved in something related to what you do. For example, my prerequisite for clients is that they are very clear about who they are and what they are selling. If they are not clear, I have several people who are business coaches whom I recommend. The business coach, then, can refer her clients to me, who are clear now on how to define their business and are ready to write their marketing speech. Website designers are another great strategic partner for me. Either before my clients write their speech or after, they will need a website. When I refer website designers, they often reciprocate and refer me.

Realtors partner with mortgage bankers. Lawyers partner with financial planners. And so it goes.

Where to Speak

Many organizations have monthly meetings, and they need speakers. Check out the Chambers, the women's associations, local service clubs with state and national affiliations, and membership organizations. Some groups need weekly speakers. Make a thorough search in your area of groups that seek out free speakers. My search has led me to travel to other chapters of the same association, and sometimes regional affiliates even if they seem far away. If the association meets at lunchtime, you can pretty much count on traffic having thinned out when you are headed for your speech and not yet started up again when you leave. Going to Orange County lunch meetings takes me the same amount of time as it does to drive to downtown Los Angeles. So don't say "no" to locations that at first seem geographically undesirable. Think of the potential benefits, and at least give it a few tries.

When you are starting out and speaking for the first time about your business, no venue is off-limits. You can speak at your child's parent meeting at the school and get clients. Parents' meetings of Girl Scouts? Boy Scouts? You never know where or when your message will land.

What to Do before You Speak

Send your client (the person who booked you for the speech) your bio and a short two-sentence description of the speech. One sentence will be from Step 1, addressing the problem of the group. Your second sentence will be from Step 2, providing your solution.

Here's an example of a speech summary:

"You never know who links to whom, so we need to be ready to 'pitch' our products and services anytime. Sharing the hard-won lessons of a thirty-year superstar career in the speaking business, Mimi will share what you need to clearly articulate your value."

Now you need to find out specifics from your client. Here's a checklist:

1. Where is the venue?

2. What is the exact time of the speech, and where does it fit into the entire meeting agenda?

3. How many are expected to attend?

4. What were the topics of speeches by former speakers?

5. How long do I have to speak? Tip: It's not always how long you're supposed to speak that matters. Meetings can start late. It's important to ask what time you're expected to quit!

The most important thing to ask for before you speak is to be copied on any mailing or handed-out flyer or *anything* they put out about your speech. Managing expectations is key. You can be brilliant, but if your topic is not the one they expect, you will fail.

What Do You Leave Behind When You Speak?

When you speak for over five minutes, always have a flyer or brochure to leave behind. Years ago, I got my first paid speeches because someone had seen my flyer on someone else's desk in their company. You never know where your material will end up. A formal "one-sheet" has three or four parts. The first is a photo. Some people will not remember exactly what you said, but they will remember your face. The second part is a short bio. (You can use information from Step 3 in the "Engage" section of this book.) The third part is a summary of the main features and benefits of your product or service (use content from Steps 4 or 5 in the "Engage" section). The fourth part of your one-sheet consists of two or three testimonials from people who are thrilled to be your customers. A speaking one-sheet highlights you as a presenter. A business one-sheet highlights your business and why people should become a client or customer. There are professionals who know how to format these one-sheets. I can help you with the words, but after that, you should have it designed, formatted, and produced by a professional.

When You Speak for Free, Can You Ask for Anything?

The simple answer is "yes." I started my speaking career by speaking for free in the evenings and weekends while I still had my day jobs. During the thirty years of running my own business, I have done some free speeches for marketing purposes, but I always define my limits. Even in this humbling economy, I still have requirements. Despite the assertive lessons from my book *Necessary Roughness: New Rules for the Contact Sport of Life*, I notice that many people are hesitant to set limits or boundaries.

I know you're not a keynoter, but here is my policy. Please take from it what you can ask for when you're being asked to speak for the joy of it.

When I accept a "freebie," there are absolute requirements. I'm very clear that if a client pays my full fee, they can have any topic they want. They can choose from among my fourteen keynotes and even more breakouts or workshop topics. However—and here's where the "necessary roughness" comes in—if it's not full fee, I require:

1. The topic is chosen by me and must be related to products I sell.

2. I must be able to sell my products at the event and distribute order forms *before* I speak to all attendees.

3. I require a six- to eight-foot product table displayed in a prominent place where participants will go—not off in another room somewhere.

4. I require at least forty minutes of speaking time. I tell them it's not a commercial; it's content. Chambers and other organizations that allow only twenty to thirty minutes always make accommodations, or I don't speak. I can speak during lunch if need be. The logic here is if you are "showing your stuff," you need *time* to show it.

5. Location corresponds to the number of attendees. If the venue is within an hour drive of my house, the audience must number at least fifty people. For a drive of more than one hour, I require at least 100 people. I *never* get on a plane for free.

6. I always require an attendee list after the speech, with names and e-mails. This is how I grow my database. For you, each speech becomes your first "touch" with every member of the audience. Sometimes it takes more than one touch to sell your product or service. You can e-mail people on your list after the speech ONCE, and send your valuable newsletter, an article, or report.

7. I *never* accept a freebie or less-than-fee speech for a large corporation with the "hope" or "promise" they will pay more next time. They never will—why should they if I *gave* my services away already? Associations are different. Each association member can go back to their respective company or organization raving about my ability. Then I can quote my real fees to their companies.

Don't be afraid to set boundaries with people who request you speak for free. You are giving *them* value, and that's priceless.

Have a Professional Introduction

When you speak for more than five minutes, have someone introduce you. They can read all the prestigious degrees you have and prestigious companies you've worked for or had as clients. That stuff is boring in a speech, and you saw there is no "step" for that in any section of this book. Moreover, the person who introduces you can do your first call to action. They can say something like, "After Mimi speaks today, you can buy her latest books and find out how she can assist you to create your perfect marketing pitch."

On the next page is your Introduction Template. All you need to do is fill in the blanks. To help you effectively plan your introduction, you can download my own introduction to use as a model at http://www.pitchperfect.biz/

Introduction Template

[Insert Your Name and Contact Information Here]

Dear [**introducer name**]: Thank you for accepting the responsibility of introducing me and creating an enthusiastic beginning for my presentation.

[**Your name**] [**verb**], [**verb**], and [**verb**] [**who you speak to**]. She frequently [**what you are best known for**]. She [**second thing you are known for**] or [**most prestigious accomplishment**].

Before starting her own [**what you do**] in [**start date**], she spent [**number**] years [**impressive past accomplishments or background dues-paying activity**].

She has a [**your degrees and education if impressive**]. [**Your name**] is [**impressive accomplishment**, **books written**, **etc.**].

After [**your name**] speaks today, you can buy [**name your books or products you have for sale**]. [**Your name**] would love to autograph her books for you.

Her new [**most recent program**] is also available to us. It contains her [**what the product consists of and how it will benefit your audience**].

When [**your name**] speaks, people [**verb**], [**verb**], and [**verb**].

Please help me welcome [**your name**].

Chapter 24
Now What?
Take Action Before You Speak

"My life is better with every year of living it."
— Rachel Maddow

So, it's your turn to speak to your networking group or the Chamber. Now you need to check two last things: the stage and your nerves.

Check the Stage

Get to the venue early to check the room—at least a half hour before the audience is seated, but I recommend a full hour just in case. Don't let a poor seating arrangement distract your audience. Be willing to move things around if there's time. Check the lighting; it may need enhancement. You may have to make nice with your host or the hotel people to change anything in the room. That's where you get to be the most charming person in the neighborhood.

Podium

The podium is the stage that you will be speaking on. Here's the definition: "A small or large platform on which a person may stand to be seen by an audience, as when making a speech or conducting an orchestra."

Get there early and walk the podium. Ask for steps if there are none. Be prepared if there are creaks or soft spots, and watch out for gaffer's tape or electric cords so that you won't trip.

Lectern

The dictionary says a lectern is "a stand with a slanted top, used to hold a book, speech, manuscript, etc., at the proper height for a reader or speaker." The lectern is about four feet high. If you are five feet in height, as I am, and you stand behind it, the audience will see you as a talking head floating above the lectern. What you can do is turn the lectern to the side and stand beside it. Then you won't be hiding behind it, and you can still look at your notes. You look brave when you don't hide behind the lectern—and it's always in your best interest to look brave, confident, and in charge.

Years ago, I was attending a Los Angeles women's conference at the Century Plaza Hotel (now the Hyatt Regency Century Plaza). Gloria Steinem was doing a keynote speech for thousands of women. There were men too, but mostly women. She was very nervous at that time in her career; however, she has a low, calm voice, so it didn't sound like she was nervous. But she was so nervous that she gripped the sides of the lectern with both hands. She built up so much energy coming out through her hands onto that lectern that in the middle of a dynamic point, she *lifted the lectern*. Her superhuman nervous energy just lifted the whole lectern an inch off the ground! And as it lifted, 4,000 people gasped. It was like witnessing a séance. They went "ooooooooohhhhh." It was distracting, and the audience giggled nervously. Of course, Ms. Steinem was well received as always because of her celebrity and brilliance.

Ever since then, I never touch the lectern or hide behind it.

Microphones

My number one rule is when there is a microphone, use it! Nothing good comes from speakers straining their voices on every word. A microphone allows you to talk in a normal tone so that you can have louds and softs, just like in a normal conversation.

The best sound comes from the handheld microphone. I know—it shouldn't be that way, given all the tricks of the trade, but that's the way it is. Besides, the newfangled mics are not available for people speaking about their businesses. These microphones are usually reserved for singers or paid keynote speakers. When you use the handheld mic, speak directly into the top of the microphone; the sides of the microphone will not project your voice at all.

If there are speakers before you, or if someone will introduce you, study the person's use of the mic. How near or far must the microphone be for the best sound quality? You can use this strategy for speaking on panels where the mic gets passed from person to person.

Last, do not be the kind of egotistical or unaware speaker who insists "everyone will hear me, no problem." Their first sentence is loud enough for everyone to hear, but then they revert to their normal tone, leaving the people in the back straining their ears or no longer paying attention.

Tips on Logistics

1. Arrive early and check out the room for outlets, view of screen, materials you will need, seating arrangements, and possible problems or distractions.

2. Always do a quick check with your visuals to make sure everything is working.

3. If using any other kind of electronic equipment, *test* it.

4. Test the mic. Request an extra battery for the microphone just in case.

5. Find the light switches and learn how they operate.

6. Always have water on the lectern. Room temperature is best for your voice, but most sites provide ice water. Drink it from a glass. Don't pull from the plastic water bottle; you are not at the gym.

7. Get the name and cell phone number of the emergency logistics person to call in case anything goes wrong.

8. Check the ventilation system for optimum temperature.

9. Check every contingency that could possibly affect your presentation.

10. If you are speaking after lunch, ask the head server to quit clearing tables once you begin.

11. If anything does go wrong, handle the emergency or distraction with as much lightness as you can. Proper humor can save a disaster and make you look downright heroic.

Check Your Nerves: Fears, Expectations, and Reality

Let's suppose you are saying to yourself, "Okay, I'm gonna do my speech in a few days. I really have problems in front of a group: I mumble. I forget. My heart pounds. My hands sweat."

You need to balance those fears or strong negative feelings with a little reality.

Reality #1. You are likely to have some preparation time for a presentation, even if it is only one day. You can rehearse it in the shower, on the way to work, or before you go to bed. Chances are great that you will have more than twenty-four hours to rehearse.

Reality #2. You do know your material. The audience trusts that you know your material. You have something worth saying. They came for your message, not a performance. They are not thinking about your nervousness. They are there to hear what you have to say.

Reality #3. No one expects you to be a Rachel Maddow, Anderson Cooper, or Stephen Colbert. They are performers who, in fact, must worry about and work on the hundreds of fine points that make for an effective television performance, e.g., resonance, timing, how to stifle a cough. They are paid precisely because of their performance skills. They need "ratings" to help sell products, promote events, and win additional contracts for themselves.

If you want to be a professional speaker, there is material for you in the bonus chapter. As a businessperson, speaking is part of your job—an important part. Your "ratings" are measured differently from those of a TV personality. Do people listen and act on what you say? Are you respected for the quality of your thinking? Are you reasonably in control of your material and yourself? Can you keep people's interest and attention?

When you can answer "yes" to these questions, then you are "performing" well in your job. An Academy Award performance? No. A professional performance? Yes! And that should be your goal: to turn in the best professional presentation performance possible.

Reality #4: You don't have to remember hundreds of do's and don'ts to be effective. You need to focus only on the three areas we covered in this book:

- Your energy and how you use it
- Your content and how you prepare, organize, and deliver it
- Your visuals and how you work with them

Reality #5: Have you ever given a presentation and thought it was not as good as you would have liked, but then people actually praised you for it? The reason for this disparity is that we all tend to be our own worst critics.

Reality #6: Finally, you still have your job or your company! That indicates your clients think you are competent, and that you are not a failure. Compare yourself to other presenters. How many of them are Academy Award caliber? Not many, I would venture.

Real Concerns

Your only real concerns should be: What works for me and what am I comfortable with?

If you are comfortable doing something, but it doesn't work for you, then you will need to learn to do that thing differently (whether it's looking at the floor or rambling on during a talk). If something works well for you (such as using humor), but you are uncomfortable doing it, then you will need to learn a technique for getting comfortable with it.

You will find everything works better when you trust yourself enough to be who you are before a group, rather than aiming to be a cardboard image of who you think you should be. No one expects you to be Anderson Cooper or Rachel Maddow, but you can take a pointer from them: they are not afraid to be who they are. Consequently, they are all different.

Those differences are a large part of what makes them good speakers. You too have a distinctive style. Discover it and you will be effective. You will also come to enjoy the experience of speaking much, much more than you do now. And the more you enjoy speaking, the more you'll be asked to do it. Effortless marketing, endless prospects, unexpected results. Yay you!

About the Author

Mimi is a superstar in the speaking business, keynoting with celebrities for audiences of thousands. Her rare combination of sophisticated humor and solid content makes her one of America's most popular funny females.

Mimi has created speeches for executives, celebrities, and entrepreneurs. She was the "pitch coach" on ABC TV's *American Inventor*, coaching the contestants to success persuading the judges and all of America. Mimi has been a visiting professor at Harvard University's Center for Public Leadership at the Kennedy School of Government.

Before starting her speaking and coaching business, she was a Human Resources Specialist with Walt Disney Company, Northrop Aircraft, and Rockwell International.

Mimi has a Bachelor's degree in Speech and Communication from the University of Iowa, and a Master's degree in Education from Teachers College, Columbia University.

She is the author of three books: *Negotiating for Dummies*, selling almost 2 million copies and translated into 6 languages, *Bless Your Stress: It Means You're Still Alive!* and *Necessary Roughness: New Rules for the Contact Sport of Life*.

To learn more about Mimi's programs and services, please visit her website at http://www.mimidonaldson.com.

Connect with Mimi Donaldson

You can find out more about Mimi Donaldson and connect with her directly here:

Email:	mimi@mimidonaldson.com
Website:	www.mimidonaldson.com
LinkedIn:	linkedin.com/in/mimidonaldson
Facebook:	https://www.facebook.com/ MeetMimiDonaldson/
Twitter:	https://twitter.com/MimiDonaldson
YouTube:	www.youtube.com/user/mimispeaks1
Mailing address:	13929 Marquesas Way, #119A, Marina del Rey, CA 90292

Acknowledgments

To my wonderful family, who encourages me and loves me and always laughs at my jokes.

To Sarina Simon, for my beautiful cover of this book! You are my bestest, always.

To Lee Ann Gradwell, who has been there from the beginning, who let me work in my pajamas and could read my most illegible scribblings. I could not have done it without you.

To Kristina Waters, whose masterful typing allowed me to march around the office, gesturing wildly and dictating the seven steps.

Special thanks to Leslie Charles, accomplished writer, for your brilliant edits.

Thank you for your contributions:

The wonderful women of NAWBO, ewomen Network, and WRS, who are my motivational speakers and my sisterhood.

The women of Manhattan Beach Professionals Association and the Santa Maria Women's Network.

The women of Temecula Women's Peer Connection, for getting me clear about my "why" story.

My cheerleaders, the band of wild, powerful women who root for me always: Sarina Simon, Pat Neubacher, Robyn Holt, Farla Binder, Lori Leyden, Lynne Romanowski, Jacki Schreiber, Ronda Ginsberg, Victoria Wilk and Cindy Wood.

And to my publisher, Robbin Simons, whose program and guidance allowed me to write this book quickly with minimal stress and maximum enjoyment.

Made in the USA
San Bernardino, CA
08 April 2016